JUDAISM GCSE RELIGIOUS ST

CONTENTS

INTRODUCTION _____ 5

JEWISH DENOMINATIONS AT A GLANCE _____ 6

PART ONE:
STUDY OF RELIGIOUS BELIEFS AND TEACHINGS _____ 8

A. BELIEFS AND TEACHINGS _____ 11

B. PRACTICES _____ 33

C. SOURCES OF WISDOM AND AUTHORITY _____ 59

D. FORMS OF EXPRESSION AND WAYS OF LIFE _____ 77

PART TWO:
TEXTUAL STUDIES AND RELIGIONS _____ 98

A. ACCOUNTS IN TEXTS _____ 100

B. THE SIGNIFICANCE, IMPORTANCE
   AND INFLUENCE OF RELIGIOUS TEXTS _____ 104

C. THE SIGNIFICANCE, IMPORTANCE
   AND INFLUENCE OF STORIES/PARABLES _____ 108

D. RELATIONSHIPS AND FAMILIES _____ 112

E. RELIGIOUS VIEWS OF THE WORLD _____ 115

F. THE EXISTENCE OF GOD _____ 117

G. RELIGION, PEACE AND CONFLICT _____ 120

H. CRIME AND PUNISHMENT _____ 122

I. DIALOGUE BETWEEN RELIGIOUS
   AND NON-RELIGIOUS BELIEFS _____ 125

J. RELIGION, HUMAN RIGHTS AND SOCIAL JUSTICE _____ 129

GLOSSARY AND FURTHER RESOURCES _____ 132

THE BOARD OF DEPUTIES OF BRITISH JEWS

HANUKIAH

INTRODUCTION

One of the biggest challenges facing Religious Education teachers today is ensuring that the information they source is both authentic and comprehensive. Many websites that carry apparently excellent material come to the subject from only one angle, denomination or approach to the religion in question. Teachers face a veritable minefield as they try to sift through which sources they can trust and which they should avoid. Many publications are written by those who have only a partial knowledge of the religion, and contain glaring errors. The problem is further compounded when these inaccuracies are repeated from book to book, with each writer replicating the misinformation from the last.

The material presented here avoids those pitfalls. It was commissioned by the Board of Deputies of British Jews, the representative body of British Jewry, and written by Clive Lawton, a leading light in the field of Religious Education. The reader can therefore be confident that this resource is an accurate representation of the way Jews practice and believe. As a rule, the traditional teachings and practices are described first, followed by the variety of contemporary approaches to be found amongst the different denominations in the UK. It provides an unbiased indication of the diversity within the Jewish community, and highlights the issues that are of most importance.

The Department for Education guidelines, on which each of the Examination Boards has designed its own syllabus, form the framework for this publication and its contents. Rather than try to adjust the material to suit each syllabus, we have provided thorough information on the guideline topics which can then be applied to any of the syllabuses, in whatever way the Examination Boards have chosen to configure their own particular preference and style.

This resource is easy to use and provides information for both students and teachers. Each topic is headed by a list of key facts, which is followed by fuller explanatory material. Vocabulary for the key facts has been carefully regulated to ensure it is easily accessible to the midrange GCSE pupil. The explanatory material is more detailed, reflecting the complexity of some of the topics, but genuine efforts have been made to ensure that all the material is comprehensible and requires limited teacher adjustment, although some pupils might need help with some sections. Teachers can use this resource to support their own teaching, in the confidence that it will help their students to meet their need to cover the range of topics expressed in the new requirements.

For those choosing the comparative themes path, we have presented short essays on each of the ten topics, comprehensively covering the fields. However, these themes are more complex and might require more teacher mediation.

In addition, there is a comprehensive glossary of terms and an easy summary of Jewish denominations.

The following material is simple enough for a student who only wishes to grasp the basic information, but also provides for the student aiming for high grades, who will find in here everything needed to become proficient in their studies of Judaism. We are confident that not only is this information accurate and wide ranging, but also written in a manner that will be directly comprehensible to and useful for hard-pressed RE teachers as they get to grips with the new GCSE requirements.

We are pleased to be able to commend to you this fine contribution that the Board of Deputies of British Jews has been able to make towards ensuring that the study of Judaism is well informed, accurately represented and, we hope, enjoyable.

THE BOARD OF DEPUTIES OF BRITISH JEWS

JEWISH RELIGIOUS DENOMINATIONS AT A GLANCE

BELOW IS A LIST OF THE JEWISH RELIGIOUS DENOMINATIONS TO BE FOUND IN THE UK. THESE DENOMINATIONS ONLY APPLY TO ASHKENAZI JEWS. SEPHARDI, YEMENITE, ITALIAN, ETHIOPIAN AND INDIAN COMMUNITIES ARE ALL ORTHODOX OR TRADITIONAL IN PRINCIPLE.

HAREDI (including Hasidim)
Sometimes, mis-called 'Ultra Orthodox' or 'Strictly Orthodox' (they are simply 'differently Orthodox') this group is most distinguished by its costume, with men wearing black coats and black hats. Haredim reject most modern ideas on evolution, changes in gender roles, fashion and permissiveness and consider the traditional codes of halachah as totally binding. There are many different sub-sets of Haredim, including various Hasidic sects, the best known of which is Chabad Lubavitch.

LIBERAL
A sector of Progressive Judaism, sometimes called 'Liberal and Progressive'. This is the most radical wing of UK religious Jewry. It is most sceptical of the authority of both the Written and Oral Torah, and is most likely to take on board contemporary outlooks in its Judaism. Until recently, Liberal Jews were the only group to accept that someone might be counted as a Jew if only their father was Jewish. Confusingly, this sector is similar to the American 'Reform'.

MASORTI
The newest and smallest denomination in the UK, allied to the American Conservative movement. Masorti means 'traditional' and this group sees itself as taking a halachic position, so it would not be right to include it amongst the Progressive denominations. However, Masorti's divergent views on halachah make it separate from the Orthodox.

ORTHODOX / MODERN ORTHODOX
The Orthodox are by far the largest grouping in the UK, but to distinguish the position of most Orthodox Jews from the Haredim (who are also Orthodox Jews) the term 'Modern Orthodox' is often used. This indicates that while these Jews also feel bound by halachah and see the Written and Oral Torahs as authoritative, they are also prepared to try to find ways to incorporate or at least learn about modern culture and ideas.

REFORM
The oldest denomination of Progressive Judaism in the UK. Reform is more tolerant of tradition than its more radical partner, the Liberals, and is therefore more likely to accommodate traditions that might seem to most Progressive Jews to have little purpose, but also which do not offend their principles. As a result, Reform is more reluctant to institute change. For example, they have only recently loosened their approach to counting people with only Jewish fathers as Jewish, but they have not yet taken up the Liberals' more permissive position.

THE BOARD OF DEPUTIES OF BRITISH JEWS

PART ONE
STUDY OF
RELIGIOUS BELIEFS
AND TEACHINGS

DECORATIVE REPRESENTATION OF THE
TEN COMMANDMENTS AT FINCHLEY UNITED SYNAGOGUE

JUDAISM GCSE RELIGIOUS STUDIES – THE DEFINITIVE RESOURCE

A BELIEFS AND TEACHINGS

B PRACTICES

C SOURCES OF WISDOM AND AUTHORITY

D FORMS OF EXPRESSION AND WAYS OF LIFE

THE BOARD OF DEPUTIES OF BRITISH JEWS

JUDAISM GCSE RELIGIOUS STUDIES – THE DEFINITIVE RESOURCE

A BELIEFS AND TEACHINGS

BELIEFS AND TEACHINGS ABOUT THE NATURE OF GOD INCLUDING GOD AS ONE, CREATOR, LAW-GIVER, JUDGE AND MERCIFUL KING

BELIEFS AND TEACHINGS ABOUT THE DIVINE PRESENCE (SHECHINAH)

BELIEFS AND TEACHINGS ABOUT THE IMPORTANCE OF THE COVENANT AT SINAI (THE TEN COMMANDMENTS), INCLUDING THE ROLE OF MOSES

BELIEFS AND TEACHINGS ABOUT THE IMPORTANCE THAT JUDAISM PLACES ON THE SANCTITY OF HUMAN LIFE, INCLUDING THE CONCEPT OF PIKUACH NEFESH

BELIEFS AND TEACHINGS ABOUT THE NATURE AND ROLE OF THE MESSIAH

BELIEFS AND TEACHINGS ABOUT THE PROMISED LAND PROMISED TO ABRAHAM AND HIS DESCENDANTS

BELIEFS AND TEACHINGS ABOUT THE KEY MORAL PRINCIPLES, INCLUDING THE RELATIONSHIP BETWEEN FREE WILL AND THE 613 MITZVOT

BELIEFS AND TEACHINGS ABOUT THE MITZVOT BETWEEN MAN AND GOD AND MITZVOT BETWEEN MAN AND MAN

BELIEFS AND TEACHINGS ABOUT LIFE AFTER DEATH, INCLUDING JUDGEMENT AND RESURRECTION

A.1 BELIEFS AND TEACHINGS ABOUT THE NATURE OF GOD INCLUDING GOD AS ONE, CREATOR, LAW-GIVER AND JUDGE

KEY POINTS

- **God as One – indivisible and unique.**
- **God created the world; all things owe their existence to God.**
- **God gave the Torah to the Jewish People.**
- **God is fair and just and requires justice and fairness.**

EXPLANATORY BACKGROUND

God is given different names that refer to different qualities. For example, Ha'Rachaman – the Merciful One, Ayn Sof – Without End, El Shaddai – God Almighty, and so on. He is addressed as 'Our Lord', 'Father', 'King', etc, but there is never any doubt that there is only one God. Even in the Torah, God has different names, the two most common being Elohim, which is usually translated as 'God', and YHVH, which is usually translated as 'Lord'. The Hebrew alphabet does not have vowels, only consonants, and so it is anyone's guess as to how the four letters YHVH are pronounced. As it is considered to be God's holiest name, Jews do not attempt to pronounce these letters, reading them instead as Adonai which means 'My Lord'. Others, however, have tried to guess the possible vowels, giving rise to suggestions like JeHoVaH or YaHVeH, but Jews do not use these. Many Jews, in following the commandment to respect God's name and not to use it carelessly, will refer to God as Ha'Shem which simply means 'The Name'. In English written texts they will substitute 'G-d' for 'God'.

The Hebrew names of God are in the plural masculine form, but Jews do not think that God is essentially male or plural. The plural form might indicate majesty, as in Queen Victoria's famous comment: "We are not amused". To use the singular would not be sufficient to encapsulate God. It might also be used to differentiate references to God from other lords or potentates.

The Jewish God has a personality and will, and is never just a 'life force' or inexorable power.

The idea that God is indivisible and unique is encapsulated in the most famous and widely used prayer, the Shema (Hebrew for 'Listen'). Taken from the Torah verse Deuteronomy 6:4 "Listen, Israel: The Lord is Our God, the Lord is One", it is more of a declaration than a prayer.

That God created the world is a clear doctrine as summed up in the Genesis narrative (Genesis 1:1-2:3), but there are different approaches to its literalness. The main concept is that God created the world deliberately and that it was good. Haredi Jews take the Genesis narrative literally, and have similar difficulties to those of some Christians when reconciling the account with current scientific theories. Most other Jews across the religious spectrum, from Modern Orthodox to Liberals, regard the narrative as a general description, not as a scientific account, but this does not mean that they take it any less seriously. It is in the Torah and there is much that can be learned from it.

The Torah comprises the first five books of the Bible. It is also known as the Pentateuch or the Five Books of Moses. It contains accounts of the creation, the origins of the Jewish People, poetic prayer and praise, and the way in which God wants Jews to relate to Him. It also contains laws and rules – the Commandments (Hebrew: 'Mitzvot'). Fulfilling the mitzvot is regarded as following God's will for the Jewish People, underpinned by the concept that the Jews should be "...holy, because I, the Lord your God, am holy." (Leviticus 20:26)

A fundamental principle is that God is just and fair. This is highlighted in the story of Sodom and Gemorrah when Abraham challenges God to be fair, since He is "...the Judge of all the world" (Genesis 18:17-32). However, as shown in the biblical Book of Job, Jews recognise that the world does not always seem fair. Over the centuries Jewish thinkers have developed ideas about life after death to square up the conviction that God operates the world on the basis of fairness and justice, even if this is not always apparent.

DIVERSITY AMONGST JEWS

There are Jews who do and do not believe in God, and there is a wide variety of attitudes towards Him. Because so much of being Jewish involves actions towards one's community and society, it may be that many 'religious' Jews do not think too much about God, and most of the time the idea is loosely in the background. "What should I do?" is more important than "What should I believe?" One small Jewish religious denomination, Reconstructionists, who are mostly found in America, have more or less avoided the idea of God and focus instead on Judaism as a religious culture.

PROBLEMS WITH THE SPECIFICATIONS

The nominated selection of God's qualities is not necessarily those that Jews would have chosen for themselves. Several key ideas are missing: first amongst these is 'Merciful', another is 'Forgiving'. Jews accentuate that God does not judge us according to His unattainable standards. He recognises that we are limited and is always prepared to listen to our repentance and take seriously our good intentions. God is also thought of as loving, protective and caring. Rabbis have commented that when Jews suffer, God weeps at their pain. A common prayer is to ask God to "...shelter us under Your wings" or to "...spread the shelter of peace over all the dwellers on earth." God is often addressed in Jewish prayer as "Our Father Who is in Heaven", summing up in a phrase both the ideas of God's intimacy and His grandeur.

A.2 BELIEFS AND TEACHINGS ABOUT THE DIVINE PRESENCE (SHECHINAH)

KEY POINTS

From the earliest accounts in the Hebrew Bible, such as God in the Garden of Eden (Genesis 3:8), or God dwelling within the portable Sanctuary (Exodus 25:8), Jews have recognised that God's presence, while indivisible, nevertheless can be especially focussed in certain places and circumstances. During Roman times, this intense Presence became known as the Shechinah, which is derived from the Hebrew word 'shochen', meaning 'to dwell' or 'to settle'.

EXPLANATORY BACKGROUND

The word Shechinah does not appear at all in the Hebrew Bible, but the concept does. The building of the Temple in Jerusalem was based on the idea that God would be prepared to somehow focus His Presence in one location, though this does not in any way imply that God is limited to or is physically trapped there. Jews have never suggested that God has a physical form that could be contained in a specific place.

In later years, Jewish mystics – the Kabbalists – took special note of the fact that the Hebrew word Shechinah is feminine, and accentuated the idea of this being the feminine aspect of God: more loving, caring and loyal, perhaps, than some of the more conventional characterisations of God as a king or a warrior. This also gave rise to ideas of some kind of union between God and the Jewish People. The sense of the intensity of God's Presence amplified this feeling of passionate engagement with Him.

Over the centuries, many have taught that God's Presence, the Shechinah, would be brought into a place by doing good things there: studying, praying, fulfilling various mitzvot, and so on. This became especially significant after the Temple was destroyed, and in a way Jews might feel that God was 'homeless'. It then fell to Jews to try and create a home for God in their own lives and places.

DIVERSITY AMONGST JEWS

As mentioned in the section on God, most Jews do not spend too much time thinking about or talking about God. Even those who do would be unlikely to talk about the Shechinah, except as a way of accentuating that good actions would receive God's approval. So a teacher might say: "Studying Torah is a mitzvah; when you study, the Shechinah will be looking over your shoulder."

In recent years, Feminist Jews have been attracted to the concept of a female dimension to God. They find it a helpful rebalancing of ideas about God, which they would argue that until now have been excessively male.

In Kabbalistic circles, popular amongst Hasidim and some others, the idea and word Shechinah might be used more commonly.

PROBLEMS WITH THE SPECIFICATIONS

Picking out the Shechinah as a special topic, and the one particular aspect of God for study here, is an idiosyncratic choice that does not reflect the way most Jews would articulate their religion or understanding of God. However, an academic analysis of Jewish sources might be justified in identifying the idea of the Shechinah as an important, but unconscious development in Jewish theological problem solving: "How can God be universal, and yet be present in a manner that allows for relationship?"

A.3 BELIEFS AND TEACHINGS ABOUT THE IMPORTANCE OF THE COVENANT AT SINAI (THE TEN COMMANDMENTS), INCLUDING THE ROLE OF MOSES

KEY POINTS

- **A covenant is a contract or agreement.**

- **According to the Bible, God had previously made one covenant with all creatures at the time of Noah (Genesis 9:8-17), and another covenant with Abraham and his descendants. The physical sign of God's Covenant with Abraham is circumcision (Genesis 17:1-13).**

- **The Covenant at Sinai was made with all the people camped there, who received the Ten Commandments and other mitzvot at the same time. (Exodus 19:5-8).**

- **This covenant, unlike the others, is conditional. It is as if God said, "If you observe My mitzvot, then I will look after you and care for you."**

- **In Jewish thought, the Covenant at Sinai is inextricably linked to the giving of the Torah, of which the Ten Commandments were only the first part.**

- **Moses was the great leader and teacher who led the Jews out of Egypt at God's command.**

EXPLANATORY BACKGROUND

The Covenant with Abraham established the concept of God having a special, unconditional relationship with Abraham's descendants. When God threatened to destroy the Jewish People after their act of gross disobedience in making a golden calf idol, Moses challenged God with this Covenant (Exodus 32:13).

This sense of unconditional commitment underpins the Jewish relationship with God.

However, the Covenant at Sinai is conditional and helps Jews understand that their failing to do what God wants might end in trouble. Jews traditionally understand the moment at Sinai as the giving of the Torah, so that God not only makes a deal with the Jews, He also spells out what they need to do, in general and in particular. The general statement is that they should be a "Kingdom of Priests and a Holy Nation" (Exodus 19:6) and the specific details are scattered throughout the Torah in the mitzvot set out there (Deuteronomy 26:16-19).

Moses is a monumental figure in the narrative of the Torah. He is the conduit through which most of the Torah is transmitted to the Jewish People. He steers them through the challenges of emerging from a slave mentality to that of a free people, and regularly confronts them with their shortcomings. But Moses himself is by no means perfect, as shown by the fact that he is punished by God for failing to follow His commands in a moment of anger.

Although no other person matches Moses in the narrative of the Jewish People, and he is considered pre-eminent amongst the prophets and leaders of the Jews, he is still only a man. When the rabbis devised the Pesach Seder service, at which the story of the Exodus is retold and discussed, Moses is only mentioned once in a brief quotation from the Torah. The point is made repeatedly that it is God who brought the Jews out of Egypt.

DIVERSITY AMONGST JEWS

Orthodox Jews have traditionally believed that the entire Torah was given at Sinai, dictated by God. It is therefore not only binding for all time, but also infinitely subtle and complex, and each line of Torah can be interpreted in many different ways. As a result of this, Orthodox Jews will study and argue about the meaning and application of what is written in the Torah. Haredi Jews are more likely to shun modern ideas and trends, while Modern Orthodox Jews regard contemporary ideas as contributing to the way they might interpret the Torah today.

Masorti/Conservative Jews hold to the same broad idea, but are prepared to accept that the text has developed over time. More importantly, they seek a greater degree of flexibility in their interpretation of the way the Torah should be applied today.

Reform and Liberal Jews, while still considering the Torah to be important and significant for Jews, do not believe that the whole Torah was given at Sinai, or even that it was all given by God. They feel that they must work out which parts are of significance today, and conversely, which parts were a product of their time and nowadays do not need to be considered.

Non-religious/secular Jews will not have any particular beliefs about this Covenant and the place of Torah in their lives. However, they may still follow many Jewish practices because they see these as culturally significant and important to their Jewish identity.

PROBLEMS WITH THE SPECIFICATIONS

For most Jews, ideas of the Covenant are nowhere near as important as the idea of the giving of the Torah, which is one of the central points of ideological dispute between diverse Jewish denominations. When most Jews think about the giving of the Torah, they do not single out the Ten Commandments from the other mitzvot. For example, many people will know of the Jewish dietary laws (Kashrut) but there is no reference to them in the Ten Commandments.

A.4 BELIEFS AND TEACHINGS ABOUT THE IMPORTANCE THAT JUDAISM PLACES ON THE SANCTITY OF HUMAN LIFE, INCLUDING THE CONCEPT OF PIKUACH NEFESH

KEY POINTS

- **Human life is considered pre-eminent amongst life forms, because humans were created Be'tzelem Elohim - in the image of God (Genesis 1:26-27).**

- **Judaism teaches that 'One who saves a life, it is as if they had saved the whole world' and similarly, 'One who destroys a life, it is as if they destroyed the whole world' (Talmud).**

- **According to the Rabbis, no-one should assume that their life is worth more than that of another. They ask: "Is your blood redder than his?" (Talmud).**

- **Generally speaking, one should break a mitzvah if it is necessary to save a life. The Hebrew for saving life is Pikuach Nefesh.**

EXPLANATORY BACKGROUND

The role of humans as the uppermost life form brings the responsibility to care for the other creatures. Jews are required to treat animals kindly This includes feeding their animals before themselves and slaughtering livestock for meat carefully and painlessly, which rules out trapping and hunting for food. It also includes allowing working beasts to remain unmuzzled to enable them to eat the produce as they work (Deuteronomy 25:4).

The rabbis teach that unlike the rest of creation, where God brought forth many creatures at a time, He made only one human at first. This informs us that every human is a whole world in themselves. Furthermore, every person deserves to be treated with the utmost respect, because humans are the only creatures made in the image of God.

This fundamental idea of equality means that according to Jewish law, one is not allowed to decide, for example, that a world class scientist is more deserving of medical treatment than a criminal. If only one patient can be treated, that decision must be made solely on the basis of which person would be most likely to benefit.

Euthenasia and suicide are utterly rejected in Judaism, because God has given someone life and it is not up to them to end it, however difficult they might consider their circumstances to be. Most Jews also feel strongly that attempting to judge a person's quality of life in order to decide whether or not they should stay alive will lead to taking a view on who is worthy of being kept alive. This flies in the face of the fundamental idea of every person being of equal and infinite value, regardless of their situation, capacity or prospects.

Nevertheless, Jewish authorities tend to be sympathetic to those who have taken their own lives. They strive to find ways to avoid judging them negatively, for example, by assuming that the suicide probably repented of their decision, but too late to pull out. In this way, the authorities avoid laying on the person who has committed suicide a stigma as great as that of a murderer, which halachah technically regards as a similar act.

Pikuach Nefesh - saving human life - is of such a high priority that if one could survive only by eating non-kosher food, this is not only allowed, it is required by Jewish law. Similarly, if lives can be saved by breaking Shabbat, then Shabbat must be broken. This is how Jewish doctors justify working on Shabbat. However, the rule of Pikuach Nefesh does not apply to a situation in which you are threatened with losing your own life unless you kill someone else. In that case, 'your blood is not redder than theirs', and you are not allowed to save your own life at the expense of theirs.

Nevertheless, if you are threatened, you may act in self-defence. This is also one of the grounds for allowing abortion. Indeed, the Mishnah is clear that although the foetus deserves care since it will become a human being, it will only become fully human when it is born. Until then, the mother's life takes precedence over the life of the unborn foetus, and the Mishnah allows abortion right up to the moment of birth, if this is necessary to save the mother.

Similarly, as long as you abide by the ethical rules of war laid down in the Torah, you may go to war. The Torah also provides for capital punishment, but only after due process of law and in order to protect the wider society. However, despite the Torah allowing capital punishment, the rabbis felt uncomfortable with it. By Roman times, they had applied so many restrictions to its use that the death penalty became almost impossible to implement.

DIVERSITY AMONGST JEWS

All Jewish views would support the outlooks and approaches set out above. However, some Progressive rabbis are starting to think about circumstances in which they feel that assisted suicide might be permissible, out of sympathy for a person in apparently intolerable circumstances. They may also take a more flexible view as to what kind of threat to the mother's health and wellbeing would justify an abortion.

PROBLEMS WITH THE SPECIFICATIONS

None – a good topic, central to Jewish thought.

A.5 BELIEFS AND TEACHINGS ABOUT THE NATURE AND ROLE OF THE MESSIAH

KEY POINTS

- **Ideas about the Messiah (which means 'anointed one') have changed over time.**

- **The word 'Messiah' was first applied to Cyrus the Great, the Persian king who in the 6th century BCE allowed the Jews to return to the Land of Israel from their exile in Babylon (Isaiah 45:1).**

- **According to Jewish teaching, the Messiah will be a remarkable human being who will inaugurate an ideal world order – the Messianic Age.**

- **Jews must help to bring about the coming of the Messiah by behaving well and improving the world.**

- **The Messiah will come either because the world has improved to the extent that it is ready for him, or because the situation for the Jews has become so bad that God intervenes and sends the Messiah to rectify this.**

EXPLANATORY BACKGROUND

There is no reference in the Torah to a messiah. The first clues appear in some writings by the prophets Isaiah and Ezekiel, but it is generally thought that these refer to contemporary events. For example, the reference to a 'child being born of a young woman who will be a great ruler' (Isaiah 7:14) is understood to predict the birth of the next king Hezekiah, who would prove to be an outstanding monarch.

During Roman times, Jewish hope grew that God would intervene by sending a leader to free them from occupation. Jesus of Nazareth was one such claimant, but there were many others. Amongst Jews, the best known was the rebel leader Bar Kochba, who was declared the Messiah by Rabbi Akiva, one of the pre-eminent rabbis of his day. When Bar Kochba's rebellion was crushed by the Romans, the Jewish response was philosophical: "We must have been wrong. We will have to keep waiting."

There were several claimants in the Middle Ages, the most famous of whom was Shabbetai Zvi, a 17th century Sephardi rabbi and kabbalist. Shabbetai Zvi persuaded nearly half of all world Jewry that he was the Messiah, and as a result, many Jews sold their possessions and packed their bags ready for the call to be gathered back into the Land of Israel. But Shabbetai Zvi converted to Islam under pressure from the Sultan of Turkey, leaving many Jews bereft and destitute. More recently, in the 20th century a number of adherents to the Hasidic group Chabad Lubavitch believed that Rebbe Menachem Mendel Schneerson, their leading teacher, was the Messiah. Uncharacteristically for Jews, some of them continue to assert that the Rebbe was the Messiah, even after his death in 1994.

Maimonides, a leading 12th century rabbi, set down the basic beliefs required of a Jew. One of his Thirteen Principles was: 'I believe in the coming of the messiah. And even though he may take time to arrive, I wait daily for his arrival'. This line, set to a haunting tune, became one of the most memorable and evocative songs sung by Jews during the Holocaust.

According to these traditional beliefs, the Messiah will be a human being, in no way divine, who will bring about a new world order of peace and justice. Different religions will continue to exist and people will retain their free will.

Another highly significant belief is that the coming of the Messiah will bring about the 'ingathering of the Exiles', ie all Jews will be able to return to live in the Promised Land, the Land of Israel. Unsurprisingly, the founding of the State of Israel was seen by some Jews as the first sign of the dawning of the Messianic Age.

Jewish teaching is not particularly clear about how this will all come about, or even what would bring the Messiah or speed up his arrival. As mentioned above, there are at least two views on this within the tradition, and for most Jews the idea of the Messiah is simply used as a means to spur them on to try to make the world a better place, or to provide them with hope when they are subject to cruelty and persecution.

DIVERSITY AMONGST JEWS

As mentioned above, the Chabad Lubavitch group of Hasidim is particularly associated with messianic fervour. Most of them have now accepted that their Rebbe was not the Messiah after all. However, this has not diminished their commitment to the messianic ideal, and they remain determined to speed up his arrival, and often speak of it.

Most Jews rarely think about the Messiah, although the idea is often used as an incentive for them to work harder towards making the world a fairer place, or simply to be more scrupulous in their Jewish practice. If they do think about the Messiah, they are more likely to think about the Messianic Age, rather than the person of the Messiah.

Progressive Jews (Reform and Liberal) have more or less rejected the concept of an individual person who will be the Messiah, and see this only as the way in which the idea of a Messianic Age would have been described in biblical times. Instead, they focus on the idea of the Messianic Age as a goal and ideal.

PROBLEMS WITH THE SPECIFICATIONS

Clearly, the idea of the Messiah is an important one in Jewish thought, but putting it here may suggest that it is more on Jewish minds than it actually is. The majority of Jews would not be able to say much about Jewish messianic beliefs.

A.6 BELIEFS AND TEACHINGS ABOUT THE PROMISED LAND PROMISED TO ABRAHAM AND HIS DESCENDANTS

KEY POINTS

- **'Israel' is another name for Abraham's grandson, Jacob. According to the Hebrew Bible (Genesis 13:14-17) the land was promised to Abraham and his descendants forever. That is why it is called 'The Land of Israel' and 'The Promised Land'.**

- **Because of this, Jews consider the whole land to be special, and it has also become known as 'The Holy Land'.**

- **The Hebrew Bible defines various boundaries for the Promised Land, and it is not easy to be sure of the extent of the land that was promised. However, the territory now called the West Bank of the River Jordan, and most of the northern part of the modern State of Israel, is certainly included.**

- **Where the Torah sets out laws about agriculture and the way in which the land should be used, these apply only to the Promised Land.**

- **The ideal place for the Jewish People to be settled is in the Land of Israel. This will take place at the time of the Messianic Age, with the 'ingathering of the Exiles'.**

- **When the Jews fail to keep their side of the Covenant to obey God's laws and follow the Torah, one of the punishments will be expulsion from their Land. But even in Exile, God will not forget the Jewish people and will eventually bring them back to the Promised Land.**

EXPLANATORY BACKGROUND

Due to current political realities in the Middle East, Israel is a difficult subject, but it must not be avoided. The place of the Land of Israel, and pre-eminently Jerusalem, is central to Jewish thought and practice. For many Jews, its significance is dominant in their consciousness of what it means to be a Jew in the 21st century.

The Land of Israel is not the same as the territory covered by the modern State of Israel. This gives rise to some of the difficulties when discussing the disputed territories of the West Bank. However, for the sake of simplicity in these notes, I shall refer to 'Israel' and the reader must bear in mind the complexities surrounding this term. Israel, as mentioned above, was originally another name for Jacob, the third patriarch after Abraham and Isaac. His children were the Children of Israel (Exodus 1:1), his descendants were the Israelites, and the land in which he lived is the Land of Israel. In Genesis, this land is referred to as Canaan, the land of the Canaanites, though again, exact boundaries are not given.

Israel is not special to Jews because of specific events that took place there, nor because of the people who lived or were buried there. In fact, some of the most significant events in the history of the Jewish people took place outside Israel: the Exodus, the giving of the Torah, the place of Moses' death, and so on. Israel is special because of this generalised promise and the Jewish sense of relationship to the whole land. In this sense, Israel is different from most other religions' holy sites around the world.

Another feature central to Jewish thought and self-identity is the Exodus from Egypt. This was not just freedom from slavery, but a promise to lead the people back to their own land, a land flowing with milk and honey - the Land of Israel (Exodus 3:8). This idea of returning from Exile to their own land became prominent when the Jews were exiled by the Babylonians in the 6th century BCE, and of course it has affected all Jewish thought since the savage exclusion of the Jews from their land, then known as the Roman Province of Judea, after the Bar Kochba revolt in 135 CE.

Even before this, wherever they might be in the world, all Jews faced towards the Temple in Jerusalem when praying. Despite the destruction of the Temple by the Romans, this practice still continues today.

At the end of the Pesach Seder service at home, one of the last songs is a prayer for a return to a renewed Jerusalem. It is also a widespread practice to sing this song at the end of the Yom Kippur service in the synagogue.

A long-standing tradition is to leave a small corner of one's home undecorated, both to express mourning for the destroyed Temple and to express the confidence that this home is only temporary, until God gathers the Jews back to their Land. A universal practice at Jewish weddings is the smashing of a wine glass by the bridegroom just as the ceremony finishes. This symbolises that, even at so happy an occasion as a wedding, Jews must never forget that the Temple has been destroyed and a moment of sadness should still be felt.

When Jews are buried, a small amount of earth from Israel is placed in their coffin, so that they are symbolically being buried in the Land of Israel.

In the 19th century, the Zionist movement picked up the Jewish yearning for return to the Land of Israel and applied to it the modern trend of national self-determination.

Since the founding of the State of Israel in 1948, many of the agricultural laws set out in the Torah have been reinstated, as Jews are once again responsible for the Land. Most notable of these is the mitzvah to let the land lie fallow for one year in seven, the Sabbatical Year (Exodus 23:10-11). This gives rise to the apparently strange practice whereby every seven years many Orthodox Jews will avoid buying Israeli agricultural produce. It also results in some Israeli farms experimenting with growing fruit and vegetables without soil, or seeking other innovative solutions to the challenge of keeping this mitzvah in a modern agricultural industry.

THE BOARD OF DEPUTIES OF BRITISH JEWS

DIVERSITY AMONGST JEWS

For some Jews, a relationship with the modern State of Israel is part of their religious understanding and beliefs; for others, it is part of their ethnic and personal identity. For a small minority, Israel plays no part in their sense of what it is to be a Jew. In the main, these are secular and usually politically left-wing Jews. However, there are also some Haredi Jews who feel that Jews should not have tried to set up the State of Israel prior to the coming of the Messiah, since the exile was a punishment from God.

PROBLEMS WITH THE SPECIFICATIONS

None. This is an important topic which is central to understanding the Jews and Judaism. It highlights the identity of Jews as a People, and not just a faith group.

A.7 BELIEFS AND TEACHINGS REGARDING KEY MORAL PRINCIPLES INCLUDING THE RELATIONSHIP BETWEEN FREE WILL AND THE 613 MITZVOT

KEY POINTS

- The 613 mitzvot is a notional number of mitzvot found in the Five Books of the Torah.

- Though some mitzvot relate to ritual matters like dietary laws or the requirement to live in a sukkah during the festival of Sukkot, a significant proportion relate to social and moral behaviour.

- Famous moral mitzvot, such as not lying or committing murder, are found in the Ten Commandments, but there are many others.

- A frequently repeated moral mitzvah in the Torah is 'Do not oppress the stranger', which appears over thirty times in slightly different wording.

- Free will is an important concept, because if one does not accept that human beings have free will, they cannot be held responsible for their behaviour.

- The Talmud says that 'Everything is in God's control, except the fear of God'. This means that people are free to choose whether or not to do what God tells them, and can be held responsible for their choices.

EXPLANATORY BACKGROUND

The concept of free will is central to the principles of the Torah. People choose the way they behave, and the Torah provides the mitzvot to give them the knowledge to make their choices.

A mystical idea in the kabbalah relates to this issue. The kabbalah claims that in order for God to create the world, He needed to make space for it – because otherwise God would fill the entire universe. This idea of God giving up some space for the world to exist, essentially withdrawing Himself, is then extended to the point of God relinquishing some of His power to allow people to have some power over themselves. It suggests that leaving people with the ability to choose is what is meant when the Torah says that God made humanity in His own image. Other animals do not have this ability to choose their actions and decide on their moral behaviour.

At the same time, the rabbis insist that God knows everything and therefore also knows how people will act. They never resolved this paradox, but insist on keeping both pieces in play. God knows what people will choose to do, but that in any given situation they also have complete freedom to decide how to act. That is why choosing whether or not to do a mitzvah has moral force.

DIVERSITY AMONGST JEWS

The various groups and denominations differ in opinion and practice as to how binding or otherwise the mitzvot of the Torah are. However, none of them disagrees that people have absolute free will, which places the responsibility on each Jew to choose to behave correctly. That is why God can hold people responsible for their behaviour. However, religious Jews all agree that God is merciful, He understands that humans are fallible and make mistakes. Repentance is always possible and forgiveness always available for the sincere penitent.

PROBLEMS WITH THE SPECIFICATIONS

This section is almost inseparable from that which follows.

A.8 BELIEFS AND TEACHINGS ABOUT MITZVOT BETWEEN MAN AND GOD AND MITZVOT BETWEEN MAN AND MAN

KEY POINTS

- **The notional '613 Mitzvot' can be divided into mitzvot between Jews and God and mitzvot between Jews and their fellow human beings.**

- **Mitzvot between Jews and God might be called ritual mitzvot, such as keeping Shabbat or Kashrut. Mitzvot between Jews and their fellows might be called social or moral, such as not lying or committing murder. The Ten Commandments include both ritual and social/moral mitzvot.**

- **Traditionally, Jewish teaching did not distinguish between the importance of the two types of mitzvah, although the ritual mitzvot do not seem to have reasons for them while the social/moral ones could be regarded as likely to exist in many organised societies.**

EXPLANATORY BACKGROUND

The reason why this text describes the 613 mitzvot as 'notional' is because although this is the traditional number of mitzvot in the Torah, attempts to list or count them result in different lists or definitions of a mitzvah. For example, the commandment: 'Remember Shabbat and keep it holy. Six days you shall work and on the seventh you shall rest...' (Exodus 20:8).

How many mitzvot do these verses contain, one or several?

However, the exact number is unimportant. Key to this section is to understand the traditional Jewish teaching that there is no distinction between, for example, keeping Shabbat and not stealing. They both appear in the Ten Commandments without any distinction, and both are requirements placed upon the Jews by God for His own ineffable reasons. So, although people may think they understand the reason for not stealing, this is not the reason for keeping the mitzvah. The reason for keeping mitzvot is not because they make sense, but because they are commandments.

When teaching and learning about Judaism, it is important not to regard the Jews as a generally law-abiding group with some special practices, but to see the whole fabric of their life, both social and ritual, as being informed by their understanding of what it means to be a Jew.

A long-standing Jewish principle is 'The law of the land is the law'. This means that Jews are bound by Jewish law to observe the laws of the country in which they live, unless those laws are utterly at odds with their conscience. As a result, people have generally seen the Jewish religion to be only about particular rituals rather than the way Jews live their lives in general. After all, if Jewish law requires a Jew to be a law-abiding citizen, most people will rarely notice that Jewish beliefs and teachings affect a Jew's moral and social life.

DIVERSITY AMONGST JEWS

In the 19th century, the rise of Reform and subsequently Liberal Judaism started to distinguish between the moral and the ritual aspects of Judaism. Early Reform Judaism argued that the ritual side of Jewish practice was rooted in ancient times and since it did not seem compatible with modern life, much of it could be set aside. More recently, however, such views have been challenged within the Progressive movements and Jews in these denominations are again recognising the way in which all the mitzvot together contribute towards a complete Jewish life and outlook on the world.

However, one major distinction between Progressive and Orthodox Jews is the degree to which they see the mitzvot as binding. Progressive Jews are more likely to have a greater variety of views on how – or even whether – to follow the mitzvot between Jews and God, than the mitzvot between Jews and their fellows.

PROBLEMS WITH THE SPECIFICATIONS

The only problem with the way this topic is expressed here is the use of the word 'man', and especially with a lower case 'm'. The Hebrew word 'Adam' means 'Man' as in 'Mankind' and is better translated to give it its full sense as 'humanity'. It certainly does not mean 'man' in the gendered sense of 'not woman'.

Furthermore, although the formulation is a proper translation of the Hebrew, Jews do not consider Jewish law to be incumbent on non-Jews. Reading this topic, some might think that Jews regard Jewish life as ideal for all humanity, but that is not the case. The rabbis identify the Seven Laws for the Sons of Noah, or the Seven Noahide Laws. These laws are regarded as the definition of a moral life that applies to all humanity, and include not murdering, not stealing, establishing a legal system and a law prohibiting animal cruelty.

That is why in the notes above, reference has been made to 'Jews and their fellows' and 'Jews and God', even though the usual Hebrew formulation uses the terms as presented in this topic.

A.9 BELIEFS AND TEACHINGS ABOUT LIFE AFTER DEATH, INCLUDING JUDGEMENT AND RESURRECTION

KEY POINTS

- **The idea of life after death does not appear in the Torah and only comes up once in the rest of the TeNaCh in one extraordinary story recounted in I Samuel 28:7-20.**

- **The absolute belief that God is just and fair, together with the clear evidence that bad things happen to good people (and vice versa), made it obvious to the Jews living in Greek and Roman times that somehow God's justice must be worked out beyond this life.**

- **Several prophets refer to some form of final judgement at the 'end of days', eg Malachi 3:19-24 in the Hebrew Bible (Malachi 4:1-5 in the Latin Vulgate).**

- **Jews grew to believe in the coming of a Messiah who would make the world a fairer place, and gather in the Jewish exiles from around the world to the Land of Israel.**

- **Certain prophets also referred to some kind of resurrection of the dead, eg Isaiah 26:19. This idea contributed to the conviction that not everything ends with death.**

- **All good people, both Jews and non-Jews, will receive their reward. The rabbis in Roman times said that 'The righteous of all nations will inherit the World to Come.'**

EXPLANATORY BACKGROUND

Maimonides, the great 12th century rabbi, included amongst his Thirteen Principles of Faith the conviction that there would be a resurrection of the dead. Another principle is that God rewards the Jews who keep the mitzvot and punishes those who do not. However, he does not refer to life after death.

Jews are generally vague about this topic and spend little time considering it. Most Jews would say that they do not know how things will work out, but assume that God is just and that things will eventually turn out to be fair. The main issue is to live a good life in the meantime.

However, various ideas have become popular over the years, and these are often turned to when a person dies or is being remembered. One such idea is that people will go to Heaven after they die. 'Heaven' is not defined, and is sometimes referred to as 'The World to Come'. In this belief, it is understood that only the soul goes to Heaven, while the body remains on Earth. The souls of good people, Jews and non-Jews alike, are believed to go directly to their reward, whereas the souls of bad people require time and prayers to help them gain access. Repentance before (and possibly even after) death can set everything straight, and those souls can also be helped if those left alive can demonstrate how the memory and influence of the deceased has affected their lives and made them behave well.

Some time in the future, the Messiah will come and improve the world, but this will not have any particular impact on the dead.

After that will come the 'Day of Judgement', when God will judge all souls, both the living and dead. At that time, those who are found to be up to standard will 'live forever in the presence of God', although that is not defined. There will also be a physical resurrection, but the way this will work is unclear and Jews do not spend much time trying to figure it out. The souls of those who are found wanting will not 'live forever in the presence of God', but no particular punishment is identified. Perhaps missing out on the reward is punishment enough, or perhaps by then all souls will have come right.

DIVERSITY AMONGST JEWS

Though most Jews, both religious and non-religious, do not spend much time thinking about these subjects, one difference of opinion – or possibly tradition – marks a difference between Orthodox and Progressive Jews.

Progressive Jews have formally rejected the idea of a physical resurrection of the dead. The practical result of this is that they do not object to cremation, whereas Orthodox Jews only allow full physical burial. However, part of the reason for this is also the conviction that it is not appropriate for people to destroy human bodies. Orthodox Jews would argue that the body is given in trust and should be returned as intact as possible.

PROBLEMS WITH THE SPECIFICATIONS

The only problem with including this topic is if it suggests that the issue is particularly important to Jews. In reality, most Jews remain fairly vague about what happens to them after they die. If they believe in God, they assume that He is just and it all works out fairly.

WOMEN RECITING THE BLESSING OVER SHABBAT CANDLES

TABLE LAID FOR PESACH SEDER

B PRACTICES

THE PUBLIC ACTS OF WORSHIP: SYNAGOGUE SERVICES

THE SIGNIFICANCE OF THE USE OF TENACH (THE WRITTEN LAW) AND TALMUD (THE ORAL LAW) IN DAILY LIFE

THE PLACE OF WORSHIP IN THE HOME AND OF PRIVATE PRAYER

THE SIGNIFICANCE OF PRAYER IN JEWISH WORSHIP INCLUDING AMIDAH – THE STANDING PRAYER

THE ROLE OF RITUALS: BIRTH CEREMONIES; BAR AND BAT MITZVAH; MARRIAGE; MOURNING RITUALS

THE IMPORTANCE OF SHABBAT IN THE HOME AND SYNAGOGUE

THE ORIGINS AND MEANINGS OF JEWISH FESTIVALS SUCH AS ROSH HASHANAH, YOM KIPPUR, PESACH, SHAVUOT AND SUKKOT

THE IMPORTANCE OF THE SYNAGOGUE; RELIGIOUS FEATURES OF SYNAGOGUES INCLUDING DESIGN, ARTEFACTS AND ASSOCIATED PRACTICES

THE ROLE OF DIETARY LAWS: KOSHER AND TREFAH, SEPARATION OF MILK AND MEAT

B1. PUBLIC ACTS OF WORSHIP: SYNAGOGUE SERVICES

KEY POINTS

- A Jew can pray anywhere, but it is preferable to pray with a community.

- There are three formal times of services on weekdays and an additional service on Shabbat.

- The Shabbat morning service is the most attended. It consists of psalms from the Hebrew Bible, various prayers composed during different periods of Jewish history and a weekly reading from the Torah. The Torah scroll is ceremoniously taken out of the cupboard (the Ark) and paraded around the synagogue before being placed on the reading desk.

- Despite there being a certain amount of ceremony during the services and readings, the atmosphere in most synagogues is relaxed and informal. Orthodox synagogues tend to have children coming and going, congregants arriving at different times during the service and people chatting to each other. Progressive services are usually shorter but more formal, and more of the service is read out loud together.

- In Orthodox synagogues, people will recite many of the prayers to themselves, with a service leader keeping everyone more or less together.

- In Orthodox synagogues, almost all the service is said in Hebrew, apart from the sermon and the prayer for the welfare of the country and its rulers. In Progressive services, a fair amount is said in English, although Hebrew is becoming more used.

- Orthodox synagogues do not use musical instruments on Shabbat and songs are sung without accompaniment. Synagogue music ranges from fine set pieces performed by the service leader to lively songs sung with great gusto by all the congregation.

- Orthodox Shabbat services use the same words every week, and regular worshippers become familiar with the prayers. Progressive services tend to use a few alternative versions, and sometimes leave opportunities for people to make up their own prayers. That is rare in an Orthodox service, but there are set prayers for almost any occasion.

EXPLANATORY BACKGROUND

The formal daily services are morning, afternoon and evening and the prayers can be said more or less at any time during those periods. On Shabbat and festivals, an additional service is added after the morning service.

In ancient times, when the Temple stood in Jerusalem, daily sacrifices used to take place. In many ways, these prayer services now substitute for those sacrifices. The additional service on Shabbat and festivals is because there used to be an additional sacrifice on those days in the Temple.

According to halachah, the full service can only be said if there is a quorum or minyan present. According to the Orthodox tradition, this must be ten males over the age of barmitzvah. According to Progressive Jews, this can be any ten Jews, male or female, over the age of majority. However, some Progressive Jews are prepared to be more relaxed about this limitation, if they have got eight or nine people present.

In an Orthodox community, if a minyan is not present, the Torah cannot be read out from the scroll, parts of prayers cannot be said, mourners cannot recite their daily mourners' prayer, and so on. Because of this restriction, strenuous efforts are made to 'make up a minyan', and even those Jewish men who are not particularly observant will understand if called upon to help 'make a minyan'.

Shabbat services are often followed by a buffet reception called a 'kiddush', at which everyone present is welcome. Kiddush is the name of a prayer to celebrate the specialness of the day, and is recited over a glass of wine or grape juice. It may also be recited, with a different blessing, over whisky or another strong drink. The buffets can be modest with cake and biscuits, or more lavish affairs with smoked salmon, pickled herrings, dips, cheese platters, etc. If someone is celebrating a special occasion, such as a barmitzvah, a birthday or a wedding anniversary, they will often sponsor the kiddush. Most importantly, the kiddush gives congregants the opportunity to socialise and chat after the service.

DIVERSITY AMONGST JEWS

Most Progressive Jews have dropped the Additional Service. They see it as backward-looking towards the Temple service, which they feel is now an out-of-date concept, with its sacrifices and priests.

Progressive services tend to be shorter than Orthodox services. At Progressive synagogues, everyone arrives at the beginning and much of the service is said together more formally than in an Orthodox service.

For other differences, see above.

PROBLEMS WITH THE SPECIFICATIONS

None

B.2 THE USE OF TENACH AND TALMUD IN DAILY LIFE

KEY POINTS

- Most Jews would not use either the TeNaCh or the Talmud in daily life. As indicated in Section C.2 (Sources of Authority), most Jews would not read the 'NaCh' part of the TeNaCh, and would tend to be most familiar with the Torah.

- However, they may well follow many daily or weekly practices which arise from commandments in the Torah or discussions in the Talmud.

- If a Jew wanted to know what to do in a particular situation with which they were not familiar, they would either ask their rabbi or consult one of the shorter codes of Jewish law, if they had the competence to understand it.

- The Talmud would be too complex to provide them with an answer, and the Torah is of little help without knowing the Oral Torah traditions arising out of any text or rule.

- Some Jews, especially Haredi Jews, value the opportunity to study Talmud as often as possible and might well set aside time to do so every day. A worldwide programme was set up in Poland, just before World War II and the Holocaust, which involves studying a daily page of Talmud, from beginning to end. The process takes about seven years, and then starts again from the beginning. People attend from all over the world, nowadays joining also by phone and internet.

- The daily prayers contain small sections from the Talmud to be read as part of the services. The central prayer that is recited twice a day – the Shema – is a collection of three key paragraphs from the Torah, including the mitzvot of tefillin, mezuzah and tzitzit.

- Some Jews have the practice of working their way through the Book of Psalms, day by day. They read at least one Psalm a day until all 150 are finished, and then start again.

EXPLANATORY BACKGROUND

Jews would only use the TeNaCh and Talmud as study texts, and Jewish study is not done on one's own. At the very least, one would find a partner so the pair can argue together about the meaning or application of the text. Jews would not sit quietly reading either the Torah or Talmud by themselves just for inspiration. Certainly, the Talmud at least is far too dense and complex for that.

As described above, a section of the Torah is read in synagogue every week on Shabbat, and a short extract of the week's section is also read at the Shabbat afternoon service and at the morning services on Mondays and Thursdays. That way, Jews do not go more than three days at a time without hearing words of the Torah read out in public. But in that context, the reading is fairly formal. It is read in Hebrew, and in its weekly sequence.

DIVERSITY AMONGST JEWS

There is no real diversity amongst Jews on this matter. Though some might spend more time than others on study, no Jews would use either the Torah or the Talmud, and certainly not the rest of the TeNaCh, on a daily basis for any purpose other than study.

PROBLEMS WITH THE SPECIFICATIONS

This is quite a strange topic and does not relate to Jewish life and practice at all.

B.3 WORSHIP IN THE HOME AND PRIVATE PRAYER

KEY POINTS

- In many ways, the home is a more important place for Jewish life than the synagogue.

- When Jewish families put mezuzot on their doors, they are performing an act of obedience to God, which makes it an act of worship. The common practice of touching and kissing the mezuzah when entering or leaving accentuates this.

- Similarly, when a family ensures that their home and kitchen follow the laws of kashrut, every meal and choice of food becomes an act of worship.

- The Jewish day begins at sunset, and Shabbat therefore begins on Friday evening and finishes on Saturday night. Shabbat and all festivals commence with the lighting of candles. This is followed by a festive evening meal, at which blessings are said over wine and bread. After the meal, a lively Grace After Meals is sung. Some families also have the custom of singing hymns around the table at the three Shabbat meals.

- A Jew can pray anywhere. Many Jews who are scrupulous about saying the daily services, but are unable to attend a synagogue, will recite those services at home or wherever they happen to be at the time. Furthermore, not all synagogues hold services every day.

- There are short blessings for every kind of occasion. There are different blessings for different kinds of food, for putting on new clothes, for seeing the ocean, for hearing thunder, for meeting Royalty, for meeting a scholar (there are different blessings for meeting scholars of Jewish learning and scholars of general learning), for hearing good news, for hearing bad news. There is even a blessing to be said after going to the toilet.

- There are often home practices for the festivals, the best known of which are on Pesach and Sukkot (see section B.7 below).

EXPLANATORY BACKGROUND

Though being together with a community is very important for prayer services, there are many other occasions when it seems appropriate to praise God or to ask Him for things. In addition, as mentioned above, the daily services can be recited anywhere, although not all the prayers can be said without a minyan.

Children are introduced to their first Jewish experiences, practices and learning at home, and the home is the primary centre for laying down important Jewish memories. The home is suffused with Jewish practices and traditions, not least of which is each of the doors having a mezuzah.

Judaism is not only a religion, but a way of life. More Jewish life takes place at home and outside the synagogue than in it. Therefore, the practising Jew will engage more with her/his Judaism at home than in the synagogue.

DIVERSITY AMONGST JEWS

For a while, Progressive Jews seemed to abandon many of the home practices, and for them Jewish life became more focused on the synagogue. That trend is now reversing, but it is still probably true that an Orthodox Jew lives a greater proportion of her/his Jewish practice at home than does a Progressive Jew.

PROBLEMS WITH THE SPECIFICATIONS

None – though the word 'worship' is a little misleading when considering the range of ways in which Jews express their religious commitments.

B.4 PRAYER IN JEWISH WORSHIP INCLUDING AMIDAH – THE STANDING PRAYER

KEY POINTS

- **Prayer in Jewish worship consists of many different kinds of material.**

- **There are prayers of praise, saying how great God is.**

- **There are prayers of thanksgiving – appreciating what God has done.**

- **There are petitionary prayers – prayers asking for things.**

- **There are inspirational prayers, to help the worshipper think along the right tracks or to prompt them to understand things better. Many of these are Psalms.**

- **There are quotations from TeNaCh and Talmud, reminding Jews of important points or ways of looking at things.**

- **There are hymns and songs, designed to lift the spirits and sum up key ideas in an attractive or poetic way.**

- **Most Jewish prayers are fixed, and most of them are in the plural first person. That means that when a Jew recites the set prayers, s/he is usually praying on behalf of all Jews, not just for her/himself.**

- **The Amidah, which means 'standing', is the central prayer of each of the daily, Shabbat and festival services. It is said while standing to attention, facing towards Jerusalem. In the synagogue, this is usually towards the Ark containing the scrolls of Torah. Many homes have a decorative plaque, called a 'Mizrach' (meaning 'East') on the wall that faces Jerusalem.**

EXPLANATORY BACKGROUND

Jewish prayer has developed over the centuries; there are prayers from every period and covering every situation. As mentioned above, ideally Jews pray together and many of the prayers are expressed on behalf of everyone. This is most apparent on the Day of Atonement, Yom Kippur, when the great prayer of confession and repentance mentions every sin one could possibly think of. The prayer is said by everyone present and each confessional statement starts with the expression: 'For the sin which we have committed by...'. Note the plural 'we'.

The Amidah also demonstrates this. On weekdays, the Amidah begins with praise, then continues with several short petitionary paragraphs asking for various things: that the sick should be healed, that justice should be done, that people should be granted wisdom, that the Jews will be 'ingathered' to the Land of Israel, that the Messiah should come soon, that God will help people repent and forgive their sins, that the land will produce good crops and, of course, that these prayers will be heard. The Amidah finishes with two or three paragraphs of thanksgiving. On Shabbat and festivals (to give God a rest, too), the Amidah starts with the same praise and ends with the same thanksgiving, but the middle section relates to the festival or Shabbat and appreciates the good fortune of having such an occasion. Nothing is requested.

The Amidah is first read privately by everyone, then if there is a minyan present, the service leader repeats the Amidah out loud for everyone to hear. The congregants do not have to stand for his repetition.

A feature of Jewish prayer, which may also be observed, is rocking. Not every Jew does this, but it is not uncommon to see Jews rocking from side to side or back and forth when praying. In addition, they will usually mouth the words they are saying and not just think them to themselves in their heads. This arises from the conviction that prayer should involve one's whole self and not just take place inside one's brain

DIVERSITY AMONGST JEWS

Once again, the main difference between Progressive and Orthodox Jews is that Progressive services are shorter and more sedate. Otherwise, most of what has been written above applies to both groups.

PROBLEMS WITH THE SPECIFICATIONS

None.

B.5 RITUALS: BIRTH CEREMONIES; BAR AND BAT MITZVAH; MARRIAGE; MOURNING RITUALS

KEY POINTS

- **When a boy is eight days old, if he is perfectly healthy, a specially trained circumciser will swiftly cut away the foreskin around his penis in fulfilment of the mitzvah in Genesis 17:10-17. At the boy's circumcision, his Jewish name is also announced, which might be the same or different to the one that appears on his birth certificate. This ceremony usually takes place at home and a celebratory party is held for family and friends.**

- **For a baby girl, usually on the Shabbat after she is born, the mother or father comes to synagogue to announce the girl's Jewish name. This too might be the same or different to the one that appears on her birth certificate. Sephardi Jews in particular also hold a party at home to celebrate the naming of a girl.**

- **When a girl reaches the age of twelve and a boy reaches thirteen, they are considered old enough to take responsibility for their own behaviour. On or soon after this birthday, the event is marked by a ceremony and celebration that takes place in synagogue with the whole community. This celebration is called 'Batmitzvah' for girls or 'Barmitzvah' for boys. It literally means 'daughter/son of the mitzvot'.**

- **Jewish marriage is a contract between two people. A Jewish wedding can take place anywhere, indoors or out, but always under a 'huppah'. This is a specially made canopy (which can just be a large piece of cloth supported on four poles) that symbolises the home the couple will make together.**

- **When a Jew dies, the body is buried as quickly as possible, preferably the same or next day. Attention then turns to the immediate family – spouse, siblings, parents, children – and a programme of comforting and support takes place.**

EXPLANATORY BACKGROUND

When circumcision takes place at such a young age, the baby hardly feels anything and recovers very quickly. Jewish babies, both boys and girls, are given Jewish names in the form of So-and-So, son of/daughter of So-and-So. Ashkenazi Jews are often named after deceased family members, while Sephardi Jews can be named after living relatives. This Jewish name never changes, even when the person marries. It is used on a Jewish marriage contract, on a divorce document, to call someone to the reading of the Torah, to say a prayer for them if they are sick, to say a memorial prayer for them after they have died and is inscribed on their tombstone. When the name is announced, it is said that this is the name by which they will be 'known in Israel' – which doesn't mean in the country of Israel, but amongst Jews.

About four hundred years ago, Jews started formally marking the time when a young boy became eligible to make up a minyan, to wear tefillin, to be called to the Torah, and so on. This is the age of barmitzvah and the celebration that marked this event likewise became known as Barmitzvah. It is usually celebrated by the boy performing one or several of these tasks in public for the first time, demonstrating that he is now eligible to be counted as an adult for the purpose of being considered responsible for his own behaviour. He is now old enough to be held accountable for keeping the mitzvot.

At that time, girls and women did not do any of these things in synagogue and no ceremony was developed to mark the age at which they became liable for their own behaviour, even though the age of batmitzvah was agreed to be twelve. However, about a hundred years ago, first Progressive Jews and then most Orthodox Jews felt that girls should also mark their coming of age. Since then, ceremonies and celebrations have been developing for the batmitzvah. In Progressive synagogues, girls mark the event at the age of thirteen and are called to the reading of the Torah, just like the boys. In Orthodox synagogues, girls usually deliver a discourse or sermon to the community, exploring something they have studied in their year of preparation. In both cases, the service is followed by a 'kiddush', a celebratory reception for all the congregation.

Marriage is a contract between two people so, strictly speaking nobody 'marries' the couple, though the expression is used. The couple marry each other. The ceremony takes place under a 'huppah' – a wedding canopy – which is often beautifully embroidered, but can be quite simple. The marriage contract, which includes provisions for what will happen in the case of divorce, is read out. The bridegroom gives the bride a ring and declares that with it, he marries her 'according to the law of Moses and Israel'. Seven blessings are sung, calling down good things on the couple and all present, and a glass of wine is shared by the couple. Finally, the bridegroom smashes a glass underfoot, demonstrating that even on this joyous occasion, Jews still remember the destroyed Temple in Jerusalem and so cannot be completely happy. The celebrations conclude with a festive meal at which the seven wedding blessings are sung again. In some families, the couple are hosted for meals over the following week, and these little parties are also marked by the singing of the seven wedding blessings.

Because marriage is a contract between the couple, divorce is technically easy. The only requirement is that the couple agree to divorce. They then go to a Beth Din, a Jewish court of law, where the rabbis/judges organise the paperwork. The divorce document is called a Get. Of course, getting a couple to agree on something when they are in the mood to divorce is often easier said than done, but no-one else can divorce them from each other. They have to agree to the divorce themselves.

When a Jew dies, the body is washed, dressed in a plain linen shroud and buried in a simple laminated chipboard coffin with rope handles. These jobs are generally performed by volunteers, and in the UK there are no commercial Jewish undertakers. Jews do not have fancy funerals or coffins. All Jews come into the world equally, and they leave equally.

Like all other Jewish prayer services, funerals are set pieces, and the service is the same at every funeral. There is no need to choose prayers, hymns or songs. Usually, someone will deliver a eulogy about the dead person. At the funeral, each mourner (immediate family) will tear a piece of clothing and wear this throughout the next week, in reflection of the biblical practice of 'rending one's garments' on hearing bad news.

After the funeral, which takes place as quickly as possible after death, attention turns to the mourners. For seven days (this period is called 'shiva' meaning either 'seven' or 'sitting') the immediate family who are mourning will sit at home on low chairs, in keeping with the biblical line about being 'brought low in grief'. They will not go out or go to work, cook for themselves, watch TV, wear make-up, or shave. They stay at home, talking about the person who has died and receiving visitors. The visitors often bring food for the mourners and talk to them of what happened, recalling their memories of the deceased, telling stories and so on. In many communities, the weekday prayer services are moved from the synagogue to the house of mourning. Only on Shabbat during this week of shiva do the mourners get up from their low chairs, go to synagogue and generally behave normally.

Mourning for parents lasts a year and for other relatives at least a month, during which the mourners avoid parties and celebrations and may remain unshaven. They daily say the mourner's prayer, which is a praise of God, perhaps at precisely the time when they are least likely to feel grateful to God. As mentioned elsewhere, this prayer is not said without a minyan, so members of the community feel responsible to help others say the mourners' prayer – which is another way of encouraging them to come to services.

Every year thereafter, on the anniversary of the death, mourners light a candle at home and go to synagogue to say the mourners' prayer. They might also go to synagogue on the nearest Shabbat to the anniversary, and after being called to the reading of the Torah they will have a memorial prayer said for the deceased.

DIVERSITY AMONGST JEWS

As in other matters, Progressive Jews have taken a divergent view on a number of the practices described above. For example, Progressive Jews are more likely to use a doctor rather than a skilled circumciser to perform a circumcision, and will hold the event in hospital. At a wedding, in keeping with their equalising the roles of men and women, both the bride and groom will give each other a ring and make the same declaration.

In mourning, Progressive Jews are less likely to have a full week of shiva and community members are less likely to visit throughout the day. Mourners are less likely to remain sitting and to a degree will organise their own lives, rather than relying entirely on others during that first week.

PROBLEMS WITH THE SPECIFICATIONS

None.

B.6 SHABBAT IN THE HOME AND SYNAGOGUE

KEY POINTS

- **Shabbat starts at sunset on Friday evening and lasts until nightfall on Saturday night.**

- **This means that its start and end times vary throughout the year. In the winter, observant Jews may need to leave work or school early in order to get home in time for the beginning of Shabbat.**

- **On Shabbat, in keeping with the mitzvah in the Torah, Jews are not meant to do any work, but instead keep the day 'holy'.**

- **In the book of Isaiah in the TeNaCh, Shabbat is called a 'pleasure' and the day should be enjoyable (Isaiah 58:13).**

- **Shabbat is a day for being with family and friends and there is much social activity: three festive meals, going to synagogue and joining the rest of the community on that day in talking, playing and relaxing.**

EXPLANATORY BACKGROUND

Shabbat is instituted in the Torah, partially as a way to remember the account of the creation that tells how God made the world and rested on the seventh day, and partially to remind the Jews that God brought them out of Egypt so that they would no longer be slaves. Both these ideas are mentioned in the mitzvah to keep Shabbat, which is the fourth of the Ten Commandments.

But saying that the Jews should not work on Shabbat and that they should keep it holy begs the question: 'What is work?' and also: 'What is holy?'

The Oral Tradition answers these questions. 'Work' does not mean effort or something that makes you tired. After all, that is not the kind of work God rested from. 'Work' in this context means creation and destruction; actions which in some way change the physical world, even if they do not involve much effort. 'Holy' in this context means making the day different and special, set aside as a time for not doing ordinary workaday things. It is a time for yourself, your family and your God.

Orthodox Jews will spend the day in sociable activity, in prayer with their community, playing games with their children, eating and drinking (but not cooking or washing up), walking not driving, talking not watching TV, meeting with family and friends, not spending time on the phone or the computer. God rested, and therefore Jews are commanded to rest – and 'rest' in this context means leaving the world alone and not trying to manipulate it. This does not mean that a Jew has to spend Shabbat in the cold and dark and not enjoy good food. It just means that everything needs to be organised by sunset on Friday. If you prepare your food to slow cook in the oven before Shabbat begins, and set your heating and lights on a time switch, you can have a pleasant day without thinking about doing anything to make things work for you on Shabbat. Similarly, if you do not drive or go shopping on Shabbat, you will need to live within walking distance of your synagogue and do all your shopping beforehand, so that you can be relaxed and worry-free on Shabbat.

Shabbat is begun by the woman of the household lighting at least two candles to symbolise the extra light and joy of the day. The Friday evening meal starts with a blessing over a glass of wine, which all share to accentuate that it is a day of celebration and pleasure. This is followed by a blessing over specially made fine bread called 'hallah', which is also shared by all present. However, it is important to note that the wine and the bread themselves are not blessed. All Jewish blessings praise God for the item or action that is the focus of the blessing. The subject of a blessing is not rendered sacred or special. In this case, the wine and bread remain just wine and bread.

On Shabbat morning, an observant family walks to synagogue where they join their community for the service and enjoy time with their friends afterwards at the Kiddush. They might also attend a learning session led by the rabbi, during or after the service. The Shabbat morning service has more ceremony than regular weekday services, especially with the centrepiece reading from the Torah.

After synagogue, people might pop into friends' homes and join them for a drink or a snack before making their way to their own home for another festive meal. They may have invited newcomers or visitors to the synagogue, and many consider it good fortune to find a guest to join them for a Shabbat meal.

Shabbat afternoon is a chance to relax; perhaps to have a snooze, play a game, go for a walk, read a book or to learn. Children will visit friends or play games with their families. Some Jews return to synagogue for the afternoon service and while there they may share a third Shabbat meal together, which will have been organised by members of the community. At that meal, which is probably more like a light snack, someone will teach something – maybe an idea drawn from that week's section of the Torah – and those present will sing Shabbat songs round the table.

Shabbat finishes at nightfall. In the UK, in summer this is quite late and there is virtually nothing left of Saturday evening. In the winter, this is very early and the whole of Saturday evening lies ahead. 'Havdalah', meaning 'Distinction', is the brief closing ceremony that ends Shabbat. It can be performed either at home or at synagogue. Another cup of wine is used – this time overflowing – to symbolise that the pleasure of Shabbat should overflow into the rest of the week. Sweet smelling spices symbolise the sweet savour of Shabbat lingering as it goes, and a plaited candle reminds those present that the end of Shabbat means the beginning of another week of work with the first thing the Bible tells us God created – light (Genesis 1:3).

DIVERSITY AMONGST JEWS

The Shabbat described above is an Orthodox Shabbat. Progressive Jews will be less concerned about the details of the rules and will more likely make the day one of pleasure and value, without worrying whether or not they drive or use the phone. Once again, the detailed system of halachah and traditional rulings will not be as influential in Progressive communities, because each Jew decides for themselves what might create the right atmosphere for them. Nevertheless, the general outline of the day will be similar and many of the practices mentioned will be identical. For example, although Shabbat might be started by the woman of the home lighting at least two candles as described, a Progressive Jewish family might start Shabbat at the same time all the year round, or wait until everyone gets home from work to begin the day.

PROBLEMS WITH THE SPECIFICATIONS

None

B.7 THE ORIGINS AND MEANING OF FESTIVALS SUCH AS ROSH HASHANAH, YOM KIPPUR, PESACH, SHAVUOT AND SUKKOT

KEY POINTS

- **Rosh Hashanah is a two day festival celebrating the Jewish New Year. It falls around September/October.**

- **Yom Kippur, the Day of Atonement, follows a little over a week later. It is a full day fast – neither eating nor drinking anything for 25 hours – and nearly all the day is spent in repentant prayer in synagogue.**

- **Pesach is the Festival of Freedom, marking the Exodus from Egypt. According to the Torah, this is when God led the Israelites out of slavery in Egypt over 3,000 years ago. Pesach takes place in the spring, around March or April.**

- **Shavuot is the Festival of Weeks, sometimes also called Pentecost (which means 'fifty' in Greek) because it takes place fifty days – seven weeks – after the Exodus from Egypt. It marks the giving of the Torah at Mount Sinai and usually falls in May or June.**

- **Sukkot is the Festival of Booths, which recalls the forty years of wandering in the desert as the Israelites made their way from Egypt to the Promised Land. It takes place five days after Yom Kippur, usually in September or October.**

- **The first two festivals, Rosh Hashanah and Yom Kippur, are together called the High Holy Days because they describe the awesome idea of God sitting in careful judgement over every human being.**

- **The next three festivals – Pesach, Shavuot and Sukkot – are called the three Pilgrim Festivals. The Torah commands that Jews should go to the Temple in Jerusalem to celebrate those festivals. Since there is no Temple any more, this mitzvah can no longer be fulfilled.**

- **The three Pilgrim Festivals are also Harvest Festivals. Pesach is the beginning of the barley harvest, Shavuot is the beginning of the wheat and fruit harvests, and Sukkot is the final harvest festival in early autumn.**

- **There are other minor festivals and fasts throughout the year, mostly commemorating events in Jewish history. These include the fast of Tisha b'Av which mourns the destruction of the Temple and other disasters to befall the Jewish people. It falls in July or August. Hanukah takes place in November or December and recalls winning back control of the Temple from pagans who had defiled it in the 2nd century BCE. Purim commemorates the averting of a plot to wipe out the Jews of the Persian Empire in about the fourth century BCE. The story of Purim is recounted in the biblical Book of Esther and this crazy carnival festival takes place in February or March.**

EXPLANATORY BACKGROUND

Rosh Hashana is celebrated as the notional day on which the world was created. The most striking feature of the festival is the blowing of the 'shofar', a ram's horn whose plaintive and primitive sound evokes powerful memories in just about every Jew. It is customary to eat honey cake and apples dipped in honey on this festival to accentuate the prayers for a sweet new year.

The Yom Kippur fast is the most demanding and solemn day of the Jewish year. It is probably the most widely observed, with the vast majority of Jews marking Yom Kippur in some way. The day is spent mostly in synagogue, making it unique amongst all Jewish events which are usually more centred on the home. The prayer services on Yom Kippur lead Jews through an intensive programme of repentance and atonement. Jews believe that if they are sincere in their repentance, they will be forgiven. However, if they have wronged another person, they must first try to make amends with that person and seek their forgiveness before turning up in synagogue on Yom Kippur to seek forgiveness from God.

One of the most famous features of Pesach, which lasts about a week, is the complete removal from the home of all 'leaven' products and their replacement with special foods that are kosher for Pesach, guaranteed to be without any leavening or yeast product. Supermarkets in areas of Jewish population may have extensive displays of special Pesach food at this time.

Many Jewish families will have completely separate kitchen utensils, crockery, cutlery, pots and pans, tablecloths and dishcloths for the week of Pesach. After cleaning the house thoroughly, everything will be changed over and the ordinary utensils put away for the week. Completely new kosher for Pesach food supplies, guaranteed by rabbis to be free of leaven products, will be brought in. In particular all bread is replaced by matzah – unleavened bread.

The other main feature of Pesach is the Seder meal that takes place on the first evening(s) of Pesach. 'Seder' (which rhymes with 'raider') means 'order' and the Seder meal consists of a service conducted round the family table at which the story of the exodus from Egypt is told with symbolic foods, like unleavened bread (matza) and bitter herbs. There are games and songs, discussions on the meaning of certain texts in the Torah, accounts of rabbinic debates on how to celebrate the festival and – in the middle of the service – a full festive meal.

Children are encouraged to take part, and one of the things they may boast about at synagogue the next morning is how late they stayed up at the Seder the night before. Besides Yom Kippur, Pesach is probably the most observed festival amongst Jews the world over. People try hard to be with their families for Pesach and the Seder, but most families are on the lookout for guests to invite to their table.

Shavuot marks the giving of the Torah, and it has become increasingly common for Jews to sit up all night learning Jewish texts and ideas, as if to relive anew the experience of receiving the Torah. Dairy foods are popular at Shavuot, with cheesecake a particular favourite for the festival.

The Festival of Sukkot lasts a week. It involves the lovely practice, which is directly commanded in the Torah (Leviticus 23: 42-43), of building temporary huts with roofs loosely covered with branches and leaves. Families eat their meals in these huts, and even sleep in them if the weather allows. This commemorates the Israelites' temporary and precarious living conditions while on their journey from Egypt to the Promised Land. This hut, or 'sukkah', is decorated with fruit and vegetables hanging from the roof, to recall that this is also a harvest festival. Many blocks of flats in Israel are designed in such a way that the balconies are not directly one above the other. That way, residents can build a small sukkah on their balcony which will be open to the sky, without being blocked by the balconies of their upstairs neighbours.

There is also the striking custom, commanded in Leviticus 23:40, to take the products of four different trees, the most noticeable of which is a long palm branch called a lulav, bind them together and wave them towards all four points of the compass as well as up and down. This practice is extremely ancient and has probably remained unchanged since earliest times. Waving the lulav is one of the few practices that directly reproduces an aspect of Temple worship that took place when the Temple still stood in Jerusalem.

The last day of Sukkot – some would say, the day after Sukkot – is the festival of Simchat Torah, the celebration of the Torah. On this day, all the scrolls of Torah are taken out of the Ark and paraded around the synagogue seven times, with much singing and dancing. On Simchat Torah, the annual cycle of reading the Torah concludes with the reading of the last section of Deuteronomy, which is immediately followed by reading the first section of Genesis in another scroll; and so the year-long process of reading the Torah starts again. In this way, Jews can say with confidence that the business of reading and studying the Torah never ends. Simchat Torah is one of the most joyous days of the year, and the general theme is that of a wedding with the Jews 'marrying' themselves to the Torah.

DIVERSITY AMONGST JEWS

Generally, all the features described above will be followed by religious Jews of every kind, with more or less attention to detail.

PROBLEMS WITH THE SPECIFICATIONS

None. It is particularly pleasing to see the most important festivals picked out, rather than the misleading practice in many syllabuses and programmes of focusing on Hanukah because it fits a cross-religious grouping of 'festivals of light', even though it is a minor festival compared to the Torah-commanded festivals listed here.

B.8 THE SYNAGOGUE; RELIGIOUS FEATURES OF SYNAGOGUES INCLUDING DESIGN, ARTEFACTS AND ASSOCIATED PRACTICES

KEY POINTS

- Synagogues can be large or small, ornate and highly decorated or very simple, but they will all have a few common features.

- At the wall facing towards Jerusalem – in the UK this is more or less the eastern wall – there will be a cupboard called the Ark in which the scrolls of Torah are kept.

- A curtain hangs in front of the Ark.

- Over, or near, the Ark there is a lamp called the 'Ner Tamid' or Everlasting Light.

- Inside the Ark are the Scrolls of Torah. Most synagogues will have more than one, and well-established synagogues might have more than ten. However, they all contain exactly the same complete text of the Torah, hand-written in Hebrew.

- The scrolls of Torah are dressed with silk or velvet covers in rich colours, often embroidered with gold thread. They may be further decorated with stainless steel, silver and sometimes even gold ornaments. These include a breastplate, a pointer and a crown or bells on the tops of the poles around which the scroll is wound.

- There are often seats of honour for the officers of the community and the rabbi, also by the eastern wall.

- There is a 'bimah', which means 'platform' or 'stage', from which the service is led and the Torah is read. This platform is usually in the middle of the synagogue, but can sometimes be at the front.

- The seating might be arranged in rows facing forward or arranged in a parliamentary style, facing around a central bimah. This accentuates that the synagogue is a place for the community to meet, not to spectate.

EXPLANATORY BACKGROUND

Many of these features echo the now destroyed Temple in Jerusalem. The Ark is a reminder of the central Holy of Holies, and the curtain is a reminder of the curtain that hung in front of it. Similarly, the Ner Tamid or Everlasting Light, is a symbol of the lamp that burned continually in the Temple. Of course, the lamp in the synagogue is not everlasting and if the bulb blows, someone just buys another one.

The decoration of the scrolls might remind one of the High Priest in the Temple. He too wore highly ornate clothing, a breastplate and a crown or turban, with bells decorating his costume. The pointer is a practical item, as the written words of Torah are not supposed to be touched. No-one wants to rub out the words in the scroll by running their finger along them. A fine pointer, often in the shape of a hand with a pointing finger, protects the handwritten text from fingermarks and possible damage.

DIVERSITY AMONGST JEWS

The only real difference between one synagogue and another, other than matters of style, taste and design, is that Orthodox synagogues have separate seating for men and women while Progressive synagogues do not. Until recently, nearly every Orthodox synagogue had a women's gallery upstairs, but now synagogues are experimenting with more creative designs that ensure that neither men nor women have better seats or a better view. These include the separate sections being put side by side, or the women's section surrounding the men's section or even alternate sections radiating out from a central bimah.

PROBLEMS WITH THE SPECIFICATIONS

None

B.9 THE ROLE OF DIETARY LAWS: KOSHER AND TREFAH, SEPARATION OF MILK AND MEAT

KEY POINTS

- 'Kosher' means 'acceptable according to Jewish law'. It does not only apply to food; for example, a badly written scroll of Torah would be 'not kosher'.

- Although 'kosher' is often mis-translated as 'clean', the concept has nothing to do with cleanliness or hygiene.

- The noun from 'kosher' is 'kashrut'; one talks of the laws of kashrut.

- 'Trefah' refers to non-kosher food. It literally means 'torn'. According to the laws of kashrut, meat must always have been carefully killed. Meat taken from an animal – including permitted animals – which has been 'torn', for example, through hunting, is not kosher. However, the word 'trefah' now means any non-kosher food.

- The main laws of kashrut can be found in the Written Torah (Leviticus 11:1-23)

- Only mammals which both chew the cud and have split hooves are kosher.

- Only fish that have both fins and scales are kosher. Therefore, nearly everything commonly called 'seafood' is not kosher.

- Various birds are identified as not kosher – mainly, but not exclusively, birds of prey. Most domestic (farm) birds are kosher.

- Almost all insects and 'swarming creatures' are not kosher. The only exception is certain types of locust.

- According to the Oral Torah, all mammals and fowl must be slaughtered in a swift and painless way, which rapidly drains the blood from the brain, rendering the animal instantly unconscious. This system of slaughtering, which can only be performed by a specially trained and qualified slaughterer, is called 'shechitah'. If animals are killed by any other method, they are trefah – not kosher.

- Fish can be killed by any method.

- All fruit and vegetables are kosher.

- Only the milk and eggs of permitted animals and birds are kosher.

- According to the Oral Torah, milk and meat products should be consumed separately.

EXPLANATORY BACKGROUND

For many Jewish people, the laws of kashrut are the most regular and conscious aspect of their observance. The requirement to keep milk and meat foods separate means leaving a certain amount of time between eating meat and milk. In UK communities, this is usually three hours. It also entails having completely separate sets of pots, pans, crockery, cutlery etc for meat and milk foods. Fish, eggs, fruit and vegetables are parev or parve (neutral) and can be eaten with either type of food. A kosher kitchen usually has separate cupboards for the different sets of utensils. There will be separate washing up bowls, brushes and tea towels which are colour coded, so that, for example, those for washing and drying 'milk' and 'meat' utensils can be told apart.

The practical effect of these rules is extensive. First of all, if you wish to make a cup of tea in a kosher kitchen, you would first need to ask which cups and teaspoons were 'milk' and which were 'meat', if you plan to put milk in your tea. If you offer to make a cup of tea for your Jewish host, they might check their watch to confirm that three hours had passed since they had eaten their meat lunch. Otherwise, they would ask for the tea to be black, or use soya milk instead, as soya milk is vegetable in origin and therefore parev. Lemon or herb teas are also commonly drunk at the end of a meat meal.

When travelling abroad, a Jew who wants to eat kosher might want to confirm that the milk they are being served has not come from a non-kosher animal. In some countries, camel's milk or horse's milk is used, and neither of those animals is kosher because the horse does not chew the cud, and neither horses nor camels have split hooves. Goat's cheese is allowed, because goats are kosher. The same goes for duck eggs, goose eggs and quail eggs. Pheasants' eggs are not kosher, because pheasants are not kosher birds.

If you invite your Jewish friend who keeps kosher to dinner, you might make an effort to ensure that you only serve them chicken (a kosher bird) and yet they still may not eat it. This could be because the chicken was not slaughtered according to the laws of kashrut.

You might be even more careful and buy your chicken from a kosher butcher who guarantees that it has been slaughtered correctly. If your friend still declines your invitation, it could be because they are uncertain about the pots you're going to cook the food in and the plates you will serve it on, as these pots and plates will have been used for non-kosher food.

Let us now imagine that you are so determined to invite your Jewish friend for supper that you actually buy a new pot to cook in and you provide plastic cutlery and paper plates which have never been used before. Surely now everything is alright? But when you serve the food, your friend refuses to eat it after all. What's gone wrong? You cooked the chicken in a lovely cream sauce – mixing milk and meat, and thus making the meal non-kosher!

As can be seen, the laws of kashrut are extensive and quite complicated. Jews who have been brought up to observe these laws find them easy and second nature, like a diabetic who has to avoid sugar, or a vegetarian who wants to avoid animal products, but for others it can seem like a nightmare.

Ensuring that food is kosher is important to Jews who observe these laws. The strictest Jews require a rabbinic authority's guarantee of kashrut on packets and tins. While one might think that a tin of beans will only contain beans and tomato sauce, some Jews might be concerned about what other food was processed in the same factory, or using the same equipment. Thus they might only buy beans which are guaranteed kosher and made in a factory that observes the laws of kashrut. This obviously makes these foods more expensive.

Other Jewish people might be prepared to eat a certain brand of beans if they can reassure themselves that the same brand's beans with pork sausages is not made on the same equipment, or that the tomato sauce does not contain non-kosher additives or preservatives. This is achieved by rabbinic supervisors visiting factories and confirming that the process fits the laws of kashrut. The horse meat scandal of a few years ago demonstrated that one cannot always be sure of what is in packaged foods.

The rabbinic authorities regularly publish lists of products on the general market that comply with the laws of kashrut. This even extends to sweets and chocolate; for example, the strong red colouring, cochineal, is made from ground-up beetles, so sweets containing this ingredient would not be kosher.

Since it is very difficult to tell one piece of meat or fowl from another, and impossible to know how it was slaughtered just by looking at it, kashrut-observant Jews will only buy meat from a kosher butcher, or in a sealed and guaranteed package. Fish species are more easily recognised, and can be killed by any method, so most Jews will buy their fish from a regular fishmongers or a supermarket.

The more one investigates, the more unexpected details emerge. For example, caviar is not kosher because it is the roe of the sturgeon fish, which is not kosher because it does not have proper scales. Sharks are not kosher because they do not have any scales, so rock salmon (which is dogfish, not actually salmon) and catfish are not kosher because they are types of shark. When turkeys were first discovered by Europeans in America, rabbis were uncertain as to whether or not they were kosher. They could not be sure whether one of the forbidden birds listed in the Torah was meant to be the turkey. Luckily for the kosher turkey industry and for American Jews at Thanksgiving, the rabbis decided that it was not on the forbidden list, and turkeys are therefore kosher.

Some Jews will eat out only in kosher restaurants, because they know that in regular restaurants, the food is prepared in pots that are also used to cook non-kosher food, and served on plates that have previously held non-kosher meals. In regular restaurants, they also cannot be certain whether the ingredients in their meal may inadvertently have in them something explicitly non-kosher. Kosher restaurants have rabbinic supervisors in their kitchens, who ensure that the laws of kashrut are properly observed. These restaurants are either 'milk' or 'meat' restaurants, so you will not get butter on your bread or milk in your coffee if you eat in a kosher steak house. These items will not be on the premises.

Many kashrut-observant Jews will eat in vegetarian restaurants, because these will not have any meat or fish. However, others will still not be confident that the restaurant is careful enough about the rules to set their minds at rest.

It can be seen from all the above material, that although pork is the most widely known non-kosher meat, it is actually no more unacceptable than any other non-kosher meat. In the Torah, pigs are not considered any more non-kosher than other animals that do not fit the requirements for kashrut. In fact, the Torah states that pigs are only non-kosher because they do not chew the cud. It would not be possible to argue that pork was more non-kosher than, for example, crab or ostrich. In fact, ostrich might be the most non-kosher of those three, as it is explicitly listed in the Written Torah as one of the birds that Jews are forbidden to eat.

DIVERSITY AMONGST JEWS

Haredi Jews will scrupulously abide by all these laws. Other religious Jews will make up their own minds about how the laws are to be applied. Even within the halachah, there is a certain amount of leeway as to how one applies the laws. Generally, Progressive Jews are less concerned with the finer details than Orthodox Jews, but that is not a hard and fast rule. If you are trying to accommodate a Jewish colleague, neighbour or friend, it is best to ask them about their own practice and to make no assumptions.

Most secular Jews will not be concerned about the laws of kashrut, but some might have been brought up to avoid certain foods and still feel that it is part of their Jewish identity to continue to avoid them.

PROBLEMS WITH THE SPECIFICATIONS

None

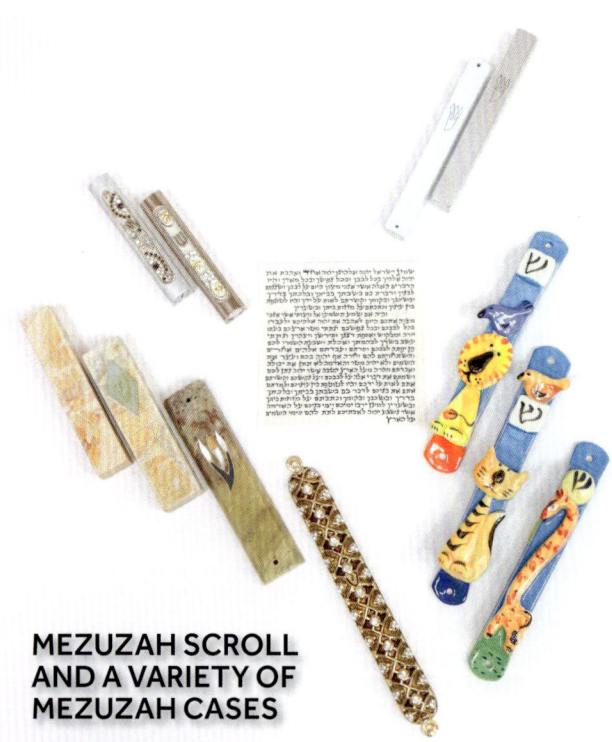

MEZUZAH SCROLL AND A VARIETY OF MEZUZAH CASES

MEZUZAH ON DOORPOST

WEARING TEFILIN FOR MORNING PRAYERS

C SOURCES OF WISDOM AND AUTHORITY

DIVERSITY OF BELIEFS REGARDING THE INTERPRETATION OF SOURCES OF WISDOM AND AUTHORITY AMONGST THE JEWISH COMMUNITY.

THE TENACH (THE WRITTEN LAW): TORAH, NEVI'IM AND KETUVIM.

THE TALMUD (THE ORAL LAW): COLLECTION OF THE MISHNAH AND GEMARAH (USE IN DAILY LIFE).

THE SIGNIFICANCE OF DIFFERENT DENOMINATIONS OF JUDAISM INCLUDING ORTHODOX (TO INCLUDE HASSIDIC AND MODERN ORTHODOX), AND LIBERAL AND REFORM (THE PLURALISTIC MOVEMENT).

PRACTICES ASSOCIATED WITH SOURCES OF AUTHORITY IN DAILY LIFE INCLUDING THE USE OF TEFILLIN, MEZUZAH AND TZITZIT.

INTERPRETATION AND APPLICATION OF SOURCES OF AUTHORITY THROUGH STUDY IN YESHIVOT AND AUTHORITY AND THE ROLE OF THE BETH DIN.

THE ROLE OF THE RABBI IN THE SYNAGOGUE AND THE COMMUNITY.

C.1 DIVERSITY OF BELIEFS REGARDING THE INTERPRETATION OF SOURCES OF WISDOM AND AUTHORITY AMONGST THE JEWISH COMMUNITY

KEY POINTS

- **All Jews agree that texts must be interpreted.**

- **Only Hasidic Jews claim that certain people – their rebbes (leading rabbis) - have the power to understand the key texts better than anyone else.**

- **Orthodox Jews are more inclined than Reform and Liberal Jews to give authority to traditional interpretations and teachings.**

EXPLANATORY BACKGROUND

For at least the last two thousand years, Jews have been discussing – even arguing – about the meaning and practical application of teachings in the Torah. More is said on this in other sections, especially on the Written and Oral Torahs, but for now it is sufficient to record that the different denominations of Judaism are almost entirely separated by their views on who can interpret the major texts of Judaism, and the way these should be interpreted.

DIVERSITY AMONGST JEWS

Because of the disagreements mentioned above, Orthodox rabbis dispute the right of Progressive rabbis to make authoritative rulings. Indeed, the Orthodox feel that as Progressive rabbis have received their qualifications from those who in their opinion do not hold the right views, they are therefore not proper rabbis. This means that key decisions taken by Progressive rabbis are disputed by Orthodox rabbis, and this invalidates, for example, conversions to Judaism, marriages, divorces and other issues of personal status performed by Progressive rabbis. Disputes around matters of personal status are probably the most intractable challenges facing the Jewish community today, and are centred on the dispute as to who is legitimately a rabbi.

PROBLEMS WITH THE SPECIFICATIONS

Most of the material that might fall under this heading is also covered elsewhere.

C.2 THE TENACH (THE WRITTEN LAW): TORAH, NEVI'IM AND KETUVIM (USE IN DAILY LIFE)

KEY POINTS

- **The Jewish or Hebrew Bible is called the TeNaCh in Hebrew.**

- **TeNaCh is an acronym made up of the initial letters of Torah, Nevi'im (Prophets) and Ketuvim (Scriptures/Writings).**

- **The TeNaCh contains the same material and books as the Christian Old Testament. However, it does not include the Apocryphal books that are incorporated by Roman Catholics and Orthodox Christians.**

EXPLANATORY BACKGROUND

Although the TeNaCh contains the same material as the Christian Old Testament, the books are arranged in a different order, which tells us something about their varying levels of importance or authority. The Christian order of the books roughly follows the chronological order of the events they describe. For example, the last book of the Christian Old Testament is the Book of Malachi, a prophet from the period of the Babylonian Exile in the 6th century BCE.

In the TeNaCh, Malachi is included in the middle section, Nevi'im (Prophets), as one of twelve books of writings by various prophets. These were grouped together because they are shorter than the three largest prophetic Books of Isaiah, Jeremiah and Ezekiel. They are often called the Minor Prophets, but only because their books are shorter, not because they are of less importance. In Jewish thought, all the Books of the Prophets are of similar status. Nevi'im also contains a number of 'history' books – the Books of Joshua, Judges, Samuel and Kings.

All the books in the Nevi'im section come after the Torah, the first five books of the Bible, which are sometimes called the Five Books of Moses or the Pentateuch (Greek for 'Five Books'). This demonstrates that the books in Nevi'im are not considered as important or authoritative as the Torah. Furthermore, the books grouped in the third section, Ketuvim (Writings), are not considered as important as those in the previous two sections, Torah and Nevi'im.

The third section, Ketuvim, includes popular books such as the Psalms, a collection of devotional poems and prayers mostly attributed to King David, and the Book of Esther that recounts the story behind the festival of Purim. Ketuvim includes some other books, for example Daniel, that Christians might expect to find in Nevi'im.

The Torah contains many mitzvot – direct commandments about the way Jews should live – as well as an account of how God created the world, and the early history of the Jewish People. Each week in synagogue a section of the Torah is read in sequence until, over a year, the whole of the Torah is read. A handwritten scroll of the Torah is used for this formal reading. It is richly dressed and ornamented, and treated with great respect. While the section is being read aloud from the scroll, members of the congregation will follow the text in a printed book called a Chumash (meaning 'Five'), which often contains an English translation, commentary and notes to help them understand the Hebrew reading.

Children learn to read and translate parts of the Torah. Even if Jews sometimes read the Torah in English, they do not forget that it was originally written in Hebrew and will want to know what the Hebrew text says. A translator can choose to interpret a sentence or section in a way that may change its meaning or provide a particular angle to the ideas contained within it, so all translations need to be treated with care.

In synagogue on Shabbat, the week's section of Torah is followed by a section from Nevi'im, which has been chosen because it echoes or throws a light on the part of the Torah that has just been read. Although these readings from Nevi'im are fixed and the same every year, they do not follow any particular sequence or thread within the prophetic book in question. For example, although several sections are read from the Book of Isaiah, they do not follow the order of that book. As a result, over the course of the year, a Jew who attends synagogue every Shabbat will have heard several sections read from the Book of Isaiah, but not in any particular order, and they may not know what is contained in the rest of the book. This practice demonstrates that Nevi'im is not considered as important as the Torah. Even fairly religious Jews are unlikely to have read most of the books of Nevi'im all the way through.

Some of the books of Ketuvim are read regularly. As mentioned above, the Book of Esther is a centrepiece of the festival of Purim and each year it is read out in full on that day. The Book of Lamentations is read every year on the fast day devoted to remembering the destruction of the Temple in Jerusalem. The Book of Ruth is read on the festival of Shavuot, and the Song of Songs is read on the festival of Pesach. Many Sephardi Jews read the Song of Songs every Friday evening as Shabbat comes in. Psalms from the Book of Psalms are used extensively in regular prayer services, and lines from the Psalms are also utilised to make up other prayers.

However, other books from the Ketuvim section are seldom read by most Jews and only those particularly interested will have read, for example, Chronicles, Daniel or Ezra.

DIVERSITY AMONGST JEWS

Many secular Jews regard the TeNaCh as a 'history' book giving the background of the Jewish People, or as a source of myths and legends, but not carrying any authority. However, they may feel proud of the important ideas the TeNaCh has given to the world.

When Reform Judaism started in the early 19th century, many Reform Jews were more interested in the ideas expressed in Nevi'im than those in the Torah. They felt that the Prophets were conveying important moral and universal messages, while the Torah was ancient and out of touch with the realities of life in modern Europe. As a result, early Reform Judaism promoted much of the Nevi'im section above the Torah, and it was common for a Reform rabbi to find his teachings and lessons in the books of the Prophets and set aside the Torah as a source of inspiration.

However, this has changed quite significantly in recent decades. Contemporary Progressive Jews have been re-evaluating their relationship with Torah, finding in it more richness than did their predecessors. They also recognise that modern Europe was not as wonderful an example of civilisation as they had previously hoped. Perhaps Jewish tradition had more to teach and offer than they had thought...

But despite this shift, it remains true that Progressive rabbis and teachers are more likely to draw lessons from Nevi'im than Orthodox teachers who will be more likely to draw their ideas from the Torah and its commentaries.

PROBLEMS WITH THE SPECIFICATIONS

It is not really accurate to call the whole TeNaCh the 'Written Torah'. Most Jews would understand the idea of the 'Written Torah' as referring to the Torah itself, the first five books of the Hebrew Bible. The Torah is the section of the TeNaCh that carries the most authority, though please note the comments above about Progressive Jewish attitudes.

C3. THE TALMUD (THE ORAL LAW): COLLECTION OF THE MISHNAH AND GEMARAH (USE IN DAILY LIFE)

KEY POINTS

- **The Talmud is a compendium of discussion and debate spanning nearly a thousand years and includes the voices of nearly a thousand rabbis.**

- **In its most popular printed form it runs to nineteen big volumes.**

- **There are two Talmuds – the Babylonian Talmud and the Jerusalem Talmud.**

- **The Talmud is made up of two sections, the Mishnah and the Gemarah.**

EXPLANATORY BACKGROUND

For a long time, Jewish teachers had been discussing exactly how one should live out the mitzvot of the Torah. For example, when the Torah says that one should not work on Shabbat, what exactly constitutes 'work'? When the Torah cites 'An eye for an eye' as a system of justice, does that mean that you have to put out someone's eye if they cause the loss of another person's? The rabbis decided that the Torah did not mean this literally, but that it was intended to be a guide to financial compensation, ie one must not try to take more compensation than the value of what had been lost. This is the same principle that exists nowadays in law, as opposed to the system in the UK until relatively recently, whereby someone could be hanged for stealing something quite small – 'A life for a purse'.

After the expulsion of the Jews from Judea by the Romans in 135 CE, Yehuda HaNasi, a great rabbi living in Galilee in the north of Israel, felt it was essential to write down the outcomes of all these discussions before they were forgotten and lost. Until then, all these ideas were remembered and passed down by word of mouth, and this was called the Oral Torah, to distinguish it from the Written Torah in the first five books of the Hebrew Bible. The book he wrote was called the Mishnah, which means the Repetition. He wanted to make it clear that he was not writing anything new, nor creating more Torah. The Mishnah consisted of six sections, each recording all the teachings and traditions concerning different topics, such as agriculture, the festivals, Shabbat and so on.

When this text became known, groups of rabbis started to discuss other items they remembered and where they thought Yehuda HaNasi had left things out. They also explored other approaches and considered different ideas concerning what he had written. These discussions took place in the great rabbinic colleges in Babylon, where there was a large and well established Jewish community dating back 600 years, and in and around the Galilee in the north of Israel. After about a hundred years in Galilee, and about three hundred years in Babylon, these discussions were collected and edited into two great compendia of discussions. Both were called Gemarah which means Completion. Each of these two Gemarahs, together with the common Mishnah, make up a Talmud, which means 'Study Text'. Thus we end up with two Talmuds. One was called the Jerusalem Talmud, because even though those who wrote and compiled it lived in Galilee, they saw themselves as the inheritors of the traditions of the Land of Israel which was centred on Jerusalem. That is where they would have been living if only they had not been excluded. This Talmud is also sometimes called the Palestinian Talmud. When the Romans expelled the Jews, they stripped the land of all signs of Jewish presence and even removed its Jewish name, Judea, and gave it a name after the ancient Philistine enemies of the Jews, Palaestina. The other Talmud was called the Babylonian Talmud, after the country in which it was compiled. When people refer to the Talmud they usually mean the Babylonian Talmud, as it is larger, more comprehensive and was the last to be completed.

The Talmud does not follow the sequence of the Torah, but discusses issues according to themes, such as the laws of damages or rules relating to fast days. It records main ideas, minority views and discussions, but rarely decides on the proper thing to do. The Talmud considers that while the Jewish People might decide to follow a particular course of action, this does not mean that other views are wrong, just that they were not accepted. As soon as the Talmud was produced, other rabbis started to write commentaries, add their ideas and explore how the views in the Talmud could be applied to their own times.

After a thousand years, a huge body of writing had developed from the Talmud, and several great rabbis of the Middle Ages wrote codes of Jewish law called Halachah. These were the agreed decisions as to how to behave, and meant that ordinary Jews did not have to work their way through the sources and discussions every time they wanted to know what to do. Even these codes were quite complicated and since then other, more simplified, codes have been written to make it easier for an ordinary Jew to know what to do in any given situation.

The idea of the Oral Torah together with the Written Torah is that they exist together. Although a decision as to what to do, for example, about heart transplants, could not have been developed until the technique existed, the simplest traditional view is that when God gave Moses the Torah at Mount Sinai, He also gave him the ability to understand how to apply the mitzvot in all different situations. In a way, the rulings of the Oral Torah originate from the same source as the Written Torah. When a rabbi qualifies, he (and, amongst Progressive Jews, she) has achieved the ability to know how to apply the mitzvot.

As a result, it would be a complete misrepresentation to think that one understood Jewish teachings by knowing only the Written Torah. In the Jewish view, the Written Torah cannot be understood without the Oral Torah and its traditions and interpretations standing by its side.

The Talmud is a record of arguments, and arguing is a classic way of learning in the Jewish world. In colleges of higher Jewish learning, the yeshivot and seminaries, it is traditional for students to pair up and intensely debate a piece of text in order to clarify their own thinking and tease out its meaning through robust argument. Indeed, the Talmud is the core and main part of the curriculum in yeshivot and in rabbinic training.

DIVERSITY AMONGST JEWS

In the early days of Reform Judaism, Progressive Jews distanced themselves from Torah study, as mentioned above. They likewise saw Talmud as mostly old fashioned and out of date, but that view has since changed.

Orthodox Jews are traditional in their approach to Talmud and its implications, mostly basing their thinking on the Talmud's lines of argument. However, some modern Orthodox Jews are starting to be more creative and flexible in their use of Talmud and other similar sources.

Masorti Jews, a fairly small group in the UK but similar to Conservative Jews in the USA, also consider themselves to be traditional. However, they are more likely, when deciding on a course of action, to base their rulings on a minority view in the Talmud if it seems to make sense to them, even though that view may originally have been rejected when the Talmud was produced.

PROBLEMS WITH THE SPECIFICATIONS

As indicated above, it is inaccurate to suggest that the Talmud on its own is 'The Oral Torah'. Although the Talmud is the original and most extensive body of Oral Torah, the Oral Torah is properly comprised of every piece of discussion and tradition in all of the texts that have been developed and are still developing around the challenge of how to understand and apply the mitzvot of the Torah to contemporary life.

C.4 DIFFERENT DENOMINATIONS OF JUDAISM INCLUDING ORTHODOX (TO INCLUDE HASIDIC AND MODERN ORTHODOX), AND LIBERAL AND REFORM (THE PLURALISTIC MOVEMENT)

KEY POINTS

- A fair proportion of modern Jews would describe themselves as not religious in any way. They are often called Secular or Cultural Jews.

- Religious Jews associate with a variety of denominations, the largest division being between those who would call themselves Orthodox and the non-Orthodox groups, most of which fall under the heading of Progressive.

- In the UK, the main religious denominations are Orthodox, Masorti (similar to American Conservative), Reform and Liberal.

- The Orthodox can be subdivided into Haredi (sometimes miscalled 'Ultra-Orthodox') and Modern (sometimes called 'Centrist') Orthodox.

- While the majority of Haredi Jews are Hasidic, not all Haredi Jews identify with the mystical and charismatic teachings and traditions of Hasidism.

EXPLANATORY BACKGROUND

Secular Jews may perform many Jewish practices and rituals, but only because they see these as part of their culture, not because of any particular belief in God or the Torah. They may also identify strongly with the Jewish People, and their Jewish identity may be very important to them. Regardless of their lack of practice or belief, no other Jew would deny that Secular Jews are Jewish, however strongly they may disapprove of the position they take. First and foremost, the Jews are a 'People' - a clan, a tribe or a huge extended family.

However, changing attitudes to the teachings of Judaism, particularly since the 19th century, have led to the development of a variety of denominations. The main split arose out of differing attitudes to the authority of the Torah, both Oral and Written. Those who feel that these are binding and that the traditions are fixed, are called 'Orthodox'. Those who feel that the Torah might be an important guide for life, but that each person must make up their own mind about how far they want to follow its teachings, fall under the heading of 'Progressive'. In the UK, the two main groups under the Progressive heading are Reform and Liberal.

Orthodox Jews can be further subdivided. Some of them feel that much of modern culture is damaging to traditional Jewish values and they strive to separate themselves as far as possible from modern influences. However, they do not reject modern technology and, for example, are happy to use mobile phones and to travel by plane.

But they are uneasy about the type of material often seen on television, or the kind of information that may come up on a smart phone or on the internet. Similarly, they distrust modern trends in fashion, feeling not only that these encourage too much concern about one's looks, but also that much of it is immodest.

These Jews are called by the general title of 'Haredi', which means 'Those who tremble in awe' – similar to the term 'Quakers'. They can often be recognised by their clothing – the women in dark colours, with long skirts and high necklines; the men with simple black jackets and coats. Some of the men wear old style black breeches and stockings, frock coats and eastern European hats, to demonstrate that they have no intention of changing with the times or keeping up with fashion. The men will often be bearded and grow long side ringlets in keeping with the mitzvah in the Torah that one should not 'cut the corners of your beard' (Leviticus 19:27).

About 80% of these Haredi Jews are Hasidim. They follow the teachings of the Ba'al Shem Tov, a charismatic mystical rabbi at the end of the 18th century, who taught that the best way to reach God was through intense passion and feeling. This was a revolutionary view at the time, and was shunned by many Jewish leaders who felt that the right way to God was through careful practice and study. But the movement spread like wildfire, especially through the poorer parts of the Jewish world in Central and Eastern Europe. Today, even amongst non-Orthodox Jews, the influences of Hasidism are widespread, with its infectious melodies, songs without words and enthusiastic dancing and celebration. Hasidim are also particularly interested in the Kabbalah, Judaism's mystical tradition; a strand of thought which has recently also captured the interest of a number of non-Jews including celebrities like Madonna.

Non-Haredi Orthodox Jews are often called 'Modern Orthodox'. Like other Orthodox Jews, they will be scrupulous about their Jewish practices, but will try to find ways to engage with the modern world: they go to the theatre and cinema, attend university, wear fashionable clothes (while still dressing modestly) and so on. It may be difficult to recognise a Modern Orthodox Jew on the street, though men might keep their heads covered either with a small round skullcap called a kippah, or another hat that may be in current fashion, such as a baseball cap or a beanie.

The difference between the two main Progressive groups, Reform and Liberal, is not often easy to detect and they share rabbis who transfer easily between different types of congregation. However, the Liberals are more progressive than the Reform; for example, it was Liberal Jews who first performed same sex marriages, and Liberal synagogues were the first to have women rabbis.

About thirty years ago, a Liberal rabbi mentioned on the radio they had eaten pork. Many Jews were outraged, but should not have been surprised. According to Liberal Jewish views, each Jew should decide for themselves what is important. Over the years, there has been a strong Progressive Jewish view that the dietary laws are now out of date, and there is no longer any need to bother with them.

Another noticeable difference between Progressive and Orthodox Jews is their attitude to the role of women in Jewish practice. According to the Orthodox tradition, women and men have different roles, with legitimate distinctions to be made between them. For example, girls come of age (Batmitzvah) at twelve years old, while boys come of age at thirteen (Barmitzvah). Similarly, men are required to say the daily prayer services, while women are exempt from this. Furthermore, and partially in commemoration of the Temple in Jerusalem, men and women sit separately in synagogue, as they did in the Temple.

Progressive Jews have equalised all of this. Men and women sit together in synagogue, no-one is required to say any of the prayer services, and both boys and girls come of age at thirteen years old.

DIVERSITY AMONGST JEWS

If one is going to explore the different groupings amongst Jews, mention should be made of Ashkenazim and Sephardim. Ashkenazim (often called German and Polish Jews) take their tradition from Northern and Eastern Europe, while Sephardim (often called Spanish and Portuguese Jews) take their tradition from the Mediterranean countries – Spain, North Africa and the Near East. Each of these two groups has a range of different traditions; even different ways of pronouncing Hebrew. Their approach to halachah can sometimes vary considerably, and they are likely to consult different codes of Jewish law to decide on a ruling. Their prayer services do not only use different melodies, but many of the prayers are in a different order.

There is a tendency to assume that all Jews fall into one or other of these two groups, but a number of Jewish communities pre-date this division of tradition. The best known of these older communities are the Yemenite Jews, Ethiopian Jews, Indian Jews and Italian Jews.

PROBLEMS WITH THE SPECIFICATIONS

The term 'Pluralistic movement' is not really one used by the Jewish world, though Progressive Jews are more comfortable with pluralism than Orthodox Jews. As the term implies, Orthodox Jews feel strongly that some positions are correct and others are wrong, while Progressive Jews are more comfortable with a wider range of diversity.

THE BOARD OF DEPUTIES OF BRITISH JEWS

C.5 PRACTICES ASSOCIATED WITH SOURCES OF AUTHORITY IN DAILY LIFE, INCLUDING THE USE OF TEFILLIN, MEZUZAH AND TZITZIT

KEY POINTS

- **Tefillin are a pair of small black leather boxes (about 3cm cubed) which contain texts from Torah. They are strapped to the head and arm as prayer aids on weekday morning services. These are usually worn by men and boys after they have reached the age of Barmitzvah.**

- **A mezuzah is a long thin case, usually about the size of a man's forefinger, containing a text from the Torah. These are fixed to the upper end of the right hand door posts in a Jewish home.**

- **Tzitzit are specially knotted and tied fringes which are attached to a four cornered garment worn during the day and especially during prayer services.**

EXPLANATORY BACKGROUND

The Torah commands that Jews should 'tie these words' to their hand and head (Deuteronomy 6:8). Traditionally, this is done by placing hand-written texts from the Torah inside small leather boxes, which are tied with leather straps on to the forehead and arm during weekday morning prayer services. The texts are written on parchment by the same craftsman scribes who write scrolls of Torah, using the same skills. In ancient times, some Jews used to wear their tefillin all day. However, it was decided that these items were too holy to be worn while going about ordinary business, and so were restricted to use only during morning prayer services. Putting on tefillin is done by men and boys over the age of barmitzvah, and is one of the things that a boy learns to do when he becomes Barmitzvah at the age of 13.

The mezuzah is also a mitzvah from the Torah (Deuteronomy 6:9). Like the tefillin, the text inside a mezuzah is hand written on parchment by a scribe, and comprises verses from the Torah that make up the Shema prayer (Deuteronomy 6:4-9 and 11:13-21). The case containing the parchment is then fixed to the upper third of the right hand door posts in a Jewish home, including the front door. Mezuzah cases can be made of anything durable – wood, plastic, glass, metal, stone, etc. Some of these are beautiful, while others are simply functional, without any decoration or noticeable design.

Tzitzit are also worn in fulfilment of a mitzvah in the Torah (Numbers 15:38-40). Although they may once have been fixed to the corners of any four-cornered piece of clothing, nowadays a special four-cornered garment is made to carry them in order to allow Jews to fulfil the mitzvah. One such garment is a kind of under-vest; an oblong piece of cloth with a hole for the head to go through and the four tzitzit tied to the corners. The tzitzit are long tassels (usually about 30 cm long) made of white wool or silk. They are tied in a specific way, with several knots at the top and eight strands hanging loose to form the tassel at the end. This garment is worn by men and boys from the age of three years old, under their shirt or top.

Although the rabbi may be the best Jewishly educated person in the community, others may be capable of leading services, and will do so. Indeed, in many Haredi communities, where all members are able to read from the Torah and lead services, the rabbi may only teach and preach. Rabbis are not priests, and there is nothing they can do in services that cannot also be done by others who know how.

In many communities, lay people might help with weddings or funerals, others might teach children for their Bat/Barmitzvah, and so on. However, the rabbi's qualification in Jewish law makes it essential that it is the rabbi who confirms that important things like marriages are properly conducted. Most people will want a rabbi to confirm that their marriage complies with Jewish law.

DIVERSITY AMONGST JEWS

Progressive Jews have both men and women rabbis, while the Orthodox only have male rabbis. However, there is one Orthodox yeshiva in America which is starting to qualify women rabbis, amid much controversy. The more Orthodox the community, the more likely it is that the rabbi will mainly be a teacher and an authority for the community, rather than serving as a minister.

PROBLEMS WITH THE SPECIFICATIONS

None

TZEDAKAH (CHARITY) BOX IN SYNAGOGUE

D FORMS OF EXPRESSION AND WAYS OF LIFE

SYMBOLISM: HOW SYMBOLS AND ARTEFACTS ARE USED IN WORSHIP INCLUDING CHANUKIAH AND MEGILLAH

EXPRESSING BELIEFS THROUGH TZEDEKAH, GEMILUT CHASSIDIM, BIKUR CHOLIM, AND TIKKUN HA OLAM – 'REPAIRING/HEALING THE WORLD' AND CHESSED – KINDNESS TO OTHERS

DIFFERENT ATTITUDES TO ZIONISM AND THE STATE OF ISRAEL AMONG JEWISH PEOPLE

THE IMPORTANCE OF NURTURE OF THE YOUNG IN THE JEWISH FAMILY

THE WORK OF ONE NATIONAL JEWISH ORGANISATION PROVIDING CARE FOR THOSE IN NEED SUCH AS IN THE RELIEF OF POVERTY AND SUFFERING, THE SUPPORT OF FAMILIES OR IN THE PROMOTION OF JEWISH LEARNING AND EDUCATION IN THE UK

THE SIGNIFICANCE AND MEANING OF AT LEAST THREE FORMS OF ART, DRAWN FROM:
- **DRAWING/PAINTING**
- **SCULPTURE**
- **MUSIC**
- **DRAMA**

D.1 SYMBOLISM: HOW SYMBOLS AND ARTEFACTS ARE USED IN WORSHIP, INCLUDING CHANUKIAH AND MEGILLAH

KEY POINTS

- A Hanukiah (Chanukiah) is an eight branched candlestick, with an additional ninth branch, used in the celebration of the eight day festival of Hanukah which falls around late November/December.

- A megillah is a scroll of the biblical Book of Esther, used during the Purim festival service.

- The most significant artefacts in Jewish practice are those containing the name of God, and the most significant of those are hand-written. Specifically, these are the scroll of Torah, tefillin and mezuzah. Also important are the printed books with God's name in them, such as prayer books and copies of the Torah or TeNaCh.

- If one of the hand-written items is dropped, it is customary to fast for a day to demonstrate one's regret. If a printed book is dropped, it is customary to kiss it after picking it up.

- The Talmud does not contain God's name, but uses other terms, such as 'Our Father in Heaven' or 'The Holy One, Blessed Be He'. It is therefore not treated with the same care and reverence as the items above. That is also true of other items in Jewish practice.

- There is a huge range of items used, many of which have been referred to elsewhere in these notes – the shofar (ram's horn), a sukkah (the loosely roofed hut), the Shabbat candlesticks, the plaited candle used at the end of Shabbat, and so on.

- All of these artefacts help to focus the attention and engage the senses – sight, sound, touch, smell and taste – to make the particular occasion more impactful and memorable.

EXPLANATORY BACKGROUND

Relevant Jewish artefacts are as likely to be found in a Jewish home as at a synagogue. As described in several other topics, Jewish life is lived and reinforced at home more than at synagogue. It is therefore not surprising that a Jewish home may have many artefacts expressing this, beginning with the mezuzah at the front door, mezuzot on interior doors, Shabbat candlesticks, a Hanukiah, prayer books, printed copies of the Torah, a Haggadah (the book of the Pesach Seder service), a finely embroidered cloth to cover the bread before grace is said and the bread shared at festive meals, and a spice holder for the Havdalah ceremony at the end of Shabbat.

The Menorah represents the Everlasting Light in the Temple. A carving of this can be seen on the Arch of Titus in Rome as one of the pieces of booty carried back by the Romans after they destroyed the Temple in Jerusalem. It is the inspiration for the eight-branched Hanukiah, although this has nine branches as an extra branch is added to hold the candle that is used to light all the others.

When Jews talk of a megillah, they are usually referring to the hand-written scroll of the Book of Esther from which the story is read in synagogue on the festival of Purim. Strictly speaking, there are five books in the last section of the TeNaCh that are called megillot (plural of megillah), but Esther is probably the best known and therefore has the name applied most frequently. On Purim, the scroll is unrolled on the reading desk, as if it had just been written. The whole book is read out, and the congregation, armed with rattles and hooters, tries to drown out every mention of the name of Haman, the villain who tried to kill all the Jews. The reading of the megillah is just one of the carnival aspects of the festival.

However, Esther is one of the only two books of the Jewish Bible that do not mention God (the other is another megillah, The Song of Songs). Without the name of God in it, a megillah is not as sacred as a scroll of Torah, or even printed prayer books and copies of the Torah. Nevertheless, it is hand-written on parchment, and is a valuable object because of the craftsmanship that has gone into it. Some Esther megillot are also beautifully illuminated and decorated, unlike the scroll of Torah, which contains only the simple text of the Torah. Most families will not have their own megillah, although they might have printed copies of the Book of Esther which they will take with them to synagogue on Purim, so that they can follow the reading.

If any item containing the name of God is damaged beyond use - even a photocopy of a text, or a newspaper article that printed the Hebrew four letter name of God - it is buried in a cemetery or stored in a special storeroom. It is not thrown away.

Other artefacts are just things. A kiddush cup is just a cup, a tallit or a kippah (skullcap) is just a piece of cloth, a Torah pointer is just a piece of silver, a mezuzah case is just a piece of plastic, etc. However, these might be treated with care and respect, both because of their associations and because they are often objects of beauty and value in their own right. They might also be family heirlooms passed down through the generations.

The Magen David is a six-pointed star, sometimes called a 'Jewish Star' and now chillingly associated with the badge that Jews were forced to wear under Nazi occupation. It became a specifically Jewish symbol fairly late in Jewish history, appearing on Jewish tombstones and buildings from the 16th or 17th century. Before then, the symbols more commonly used to represent Jews, and which can still be found in synagogue decoration today, are the seven-branched candlestick (the Menorah) and a representation of the two tablets of stone on which, according to the Torah, the Ten Commandments were written by God. No-one knows what these might have actually looked like.

In modern Israel, the Magen David has been reclaimed from its negative associations with the Holocaust to become the central symbol on the national flag, while the seven-branched Menorah has become the symbol of the government of Israel. Many Jews might wear a Magen David necklace. This carries no religious significance, although the wearer might feel it to be an important statement about their Jewish identity.

DIVERSITY AMONGST JEWS

Individual Jews will feel differently about different objects, but overall, all that has been said above will reflect the general approach by all types of Jew to artefacts and objects.

PROBLEMS WITH THE SPECIFICATIONS

The specific selection of the two named items is puzzling. But the overall topic deserves attention, and a knowledge of the various artefacts that might be found in Jewish homes and synagogues will give a richer, deeper insight into Jewish life as it is lived.

D.2 EXPRESSING BELIEFS THROUGH TZEDEKAH, GEMILUT CHASSIDIM, BIKUR CHOLIM AND TIKKUN HA OLAM – 'REPAIRING/HEALING THE WORLD' AND CHESSED – KINDNESS TO OTHERS

KEY POINTS

- 'Tzedakah' is poorly translated as 'charity' and 'Gemilut Chassadim' can be translated as 'acts of kindness'. (NB There are mis-spellings in the DfE guideline above)

- Tzedakah comes from the Hebrew word 'Tzedek' which means 'justice', and the derived idea – tzedakah - has more to do with being fair than being generous. Thus giving tzedakah is a duty, not a choice.

- Gemilut Chassadim is the mirror image of tzedakah. While tzedakah is the giving of your resources – money and objects – Gemilut Chassadim is giving of yourself.

- Forms of Gemilut Chassadim include burying the dead, comforting mourners, visiting the sick, giving time to the needy, and so on.

- Bikur Cholim (the 'ch' is guttural as in 'loch') is the mitzvah of visiting the sick. One of the main hospitals in Jerusalem is called 'Bikur Cholim' after this mitzvah.

- By extension, Bikur Cholim has now come to refer to the whole field of healing and medicine.

- Jewish communities often establish a fund or service called 'Bikur Cholim' to cater for the needs of the sick.

- The Torah relates that while Abraham is recuperating from circumcising himself, God speaks to him (Genesis 17:26-18:1). Jewish tradition learns from this that even God visits the sick.

- Tikkun Ha'Olam – or, more frequently, Tikkun Olam – means 'healing/repairing the world'. This was originally a kabbalistic concept, whereby Jews tried hard to keep the mitzvot in the hope of rebalancing the world with their good deeds, thus encouraging God to restore the world to His original ideal creation.

- In recent years, Tikkun Olam has come to refer more and more to activities that might fall under the heading of social justice projects and environmental work.

- Both the original meaning of the term Tikkun Olam, and its more modern application, make clear the Jewish conviction that the world is basically a good place and that God expects people, especially Jews, to be His allies in restoring order when things have gone wrong.

- **Chessed (kindness) is related to the word 'Hasid' as in the Jewish movement called 'Hasidism'. Hasid means 'pious/religious one' and it is noteworthy that the word for 'kindness' and the word for 'religious' are connected. This is another demonstration that in Jewish thought religion is not so much about what you believe as about the way you behave.**

EXPLANATORY BACKGROUND

The great 12th century rabbi, Moses Maimonides, outlined several levels of giving tzedakah ranging from grudgingly giving less than you should, up to the highest ideal of taking a poor person into partnership. Ideally, tzedakah should take into account the recipient's dignity and self-respect, and recipients should not be demeaned or even expected to feel grateful.

However, there is a limit to giving tzedakah. Usually one should give about 10% of one's disposable income, but certainly not make oneself poor by giving. That would be foolish. Obviously, very rich people can afford to – and should – give far more than 10%.

Tzedakah is a widespread practice within the Jewish community. Jews not only provide extensive charitable services to cater for the poor and needy in their own community - homes for the elderly, mental health support, cancer care, welfare for troubled families, special educational provision and so on - but are also generous donors to general causes. A glance at the patrons of medical research charities or the plaques on art galleries, concert halls, universities and the like will reveal a disproportionate number of Jewish names.

The rabbis say that the world is built on three things: Torah, Avodah (worship) and Gemilut Chassadim, so this is seen as a central pillar of how the world and a good society work. Both Tzedakah and Gemilut Chassadim are ways of rebalancing the world which God created as 'good' but which can become unbalanced through human misfortune or misbehaviour.

The rabbis have commented that when God says at the moment of creating humanity "Let us make Man in our own image", He might be calling on human beings to help Him to achieve that goal. Similarly, the Torah recognises that over time, some people can become poor and others rich, and legislates a remarkable idea – that every fifty years all land should be returned to its original tribal owners. We do not know exactly how this worked in practice, but the very idea makes it clear that people continuously need to improve the world by their action, because things can very quickly become unequal.

The increasingly popular 'Mitzvah Day' is a perfect example of thousands of Jews in the UK doing Gemilut Chassadim. On this day – usually a Sunday in November - Jews organise themselves to do all kinds of acts to help others. They might clean up a park, paint the flats of the elderly, or collect food at a supermarket for a homeless shelter. They might organise a party for children who do not usually get to enjoy such a thing, or pack parcels of essentials and small luxuries for asylum seekers and refugees. There are dozens of creative ideas for making the world a better place. Many of the projects started on Mitzvah Day continue all year round. Other communities have been inspired by Mitzvah Day; Hindus have created their own 'Sewa Day' and many churches and Muslim communities now join in on Mitzvah Day. The inter-community working is also its own piece of Gemilut Chassadim. (See elsewhere for 'Tikkun Olam'.)

Both fields of mitzvah – Tzedakah and Gemilut Chassadim - are also robust answers to the very early question that according to the Torah, one of the earliest human beings asked God. After Adam and Eve's son Cain has killed his brother Abel, God asks him, 'Where is your brother?' Cain replies, 'Am I my brother's keeper?' The unequivocal answer in these Jewish commandments is: 'Yes, of course you are,' and in the famous phrase 'There, but for the grace of God, go I.' Jews might add to that: 'And also, by the grace of my fellow human beings.'

Bikur Cholim is a sub-set of Gemilut Chassadim and is one way of performing that mitzvah. This is an example of a mitzvah where the halachah has not prescribed any quantities or limits. Even a brief visit to a sick person fulfils the mitzvah; any amount of visiting does not satisfy what might be done. Usually the halachah is quite precise about what exactly a Jew has to do to fulfil a mitzvah.

Bikur Cholim is a good example of how a mitzvah is 'learnt out' of the Written Torah. Nowhere does it say 'You must visit the sick', but as mentioned above, the rabbis note that God visited Abraham while he was recuperating from his circumcision. God could have waited until Abaraham was fully recovered, but did not do so. From this, the rabbis learned that visiting the sick is a virtuous action, and so it was 'learnt out' as a mitzvah in the Oral Torah, even though it was not explicitly set down in the Written Torah. Indeed, in the Talmud it is claimed that a person who visits the sick helps them to recover, while a person who does not contributes to their deterioration.

The Torah mostly legislates for the behaviour between one Jew and another, and it might be assumed that most Jews, especially when Jews were shunned by other people, would be likely to visit fellow Jews who were sick. Back in the day, it was quite probable that they did not know any non-Jews socially. Nevertheless, the Talmud teaches that when a Jew visits his sick friend, he should also visit sick non-Jewish people. Thus a person who knows how to do Bikur Cholim properly might visit a friend in hospital, but will also stop off at each of the other beds on the ward to ask how the other patients are feeling, and to give them a kind word.

This original fairly limited concept as to how to give comfort and relief to sick people has grown into the whole field of medical science. For many centuries, Jews have been famed for their medical work. For example, the great 12th century rabbi Maimonides was doctor to the court of Saladin in Cairo. As a result, the halachah has developed extensive rulings and views about modern medical ethical dilemmas, such as end of life concerns, transplants, artificial insemination and so on. Overall, the Jewish approach to medical advance is that it is positive, arising from the root concept that helping the sick is a good thing.

Though Tikkun Olam had long been a concept in Jewish thought, it used to be fairly esoteric and mostly of interest to the minority engaged in kabbalistic ideas. However, in or around the 1960s, Progressive Jews took up the idea and applied it to their extensive involvement in the American Civil Rights movement and, from that, to all kinds of social action activities. The idea that Jews should work to improve the world is deeply embedded in Jewish thought, but this took it outside the simple fulfilling of mitzvot and extended it to mean that a Jewish person should also become involved in popular (or unpopular) social issues.

Such beliefs make clear that despite a long history of mistreatment and disadvantage, Jews are an optimistic activist group. They recognise their responsibility to improve the world, and believe that it is possible to do so.

For a couple of decades, Orthodox Jews hung back on this idea, fearing that the Progressive Jews were trying to find some kind of practice that was not necessarily rooted in the Torah. However, since the 1980s and 90s, more and more Orthodox leaders and rabbis have espoused social action work as falling under the heading of Tikkun Olam.

For example, during the asylum seeker crisis in the summer of 2015, the Orthodox Chief Rabbi of the UK led a delegation of Orthodox rabbis to a refugee reception centre to see what could be done to help. Meanwhile, the Jewish charity World Jewish Relief raised over three quarters of a million pounds to aid the asylum seekers. Many – possibly most – Jews in the UK will also have donated to the general appeals for this cause, so the £750,000 raised by World Jewish Relief is only a proportion of what the quarter of a million Jews in the UK will have given to just this one issue.

Chessed is the quality that encourages one to give Tzedakah generously and to do Gemilut Chassadim. To show chessed is considered beautiful, because one is not just dutifully performing the acts sufficient to fulfil the relevant mitzvot, but doing so with care and concern in one's heart.

DIVERSITY AMONGST JEWS

There is no real disagreement amongst Jews on these topics, except perhaps that the more inward-looking sections of the Jewish community, the Haredim, are more likely to do Tzedakah and Gemilut Chassadim within their own community, and Progressive Jews might devote more time to joining in with general causes.

As outlined in other topics, Judaism is more a religion of 'deed' than 'creed' – it is more about what you do than what you believe. Many Jews may not think too much about their beliefs most of the time, even if they are quite observant in their practices. Some of these social mitzvot are also so deeply engrained in Jewish behaviour that even non-religious Jews might see behaving in such a way as simply expressing their 'Jewish identity'. They would argue that one of the essential features of the Jews, whether they are religious or not, is a desire to work for the good of society.

Because of the very new nature of some of the emerging medical challenges, this is an area where Jews are likely to disagree about the right thing to do in a given situation. Even Orthodox rabbis will disagree with each other. It will take time for the consensus halachah to emerge from the variety of different views as to how to apply ancient ideas and principles to brand new possibilities and problems.

PROBLEMS WITH THE SPECIFICATIONS

This is an important reminder that being a committed Jew is about more than just a series of distinctive rituals. Mitzvot between Jews and their fellow human beings are equally important. It is a shame that the words are mis-spelled, but it is far more important that students should know the concepts and practices, rather than struggle too hard to learn some potentially difficult Hebrew words. Many British Jews will also more comfortably use the usual English terms like 'charity' and 'doing good' rather than reach for the proper Hebrew terms for these mitzvot.

D.3 DIFFERENT ATTITUDES TO ZIONISM AND THE STATE OF ISRAEL AMONG JEWISH PEOPLE

KEY POINTS

- Zionism is the belief that Jews have a right to their own independent country in the Land of Israel. A Zionist is someone who believes in this right.

- Most Jews are Zionists, though that does not mean that they necessarily agree with the policies of any particular Israeli politician or government. Similarly, someone can be a loyal British citizen while opposing the policies of any particular government.

- Most Modern Orthodox Jews support and care about the State of Israel. Many will have family members living there. This is also increasingly true about Progressive Jews.

- Originally, most Progressive Jews felt uneasy about Zionism and even opposed it, because they thought that Jews should try to integrate in the countries in which they lived. They believed that if Jews did this well enough, anti-Jewish prejudice – antisemitism – would die out.

- After the Holocaust, and subsequently after the close call Israel suffered in the Six Day War of 1967, when her Arab neighbours attempted to wipe it out, most Progressive Jews changed their minds and became increasingly supportive of the right of – and need for – Israel to exist.

- Haredi Jews are mostly indifferent as to whether or not there should be a political state of Israel. However, many Haredim live in Israel and play their part in the politics of the state in the same way as they might in any other country.

- A tiny number of Haredim actively oppose the State of Israel, believing that its existence is against God's will. God exiled the Jewish People, and they feel it would be wrong to re-establish a government in Israel until God has granted permission.

- Secular Jews hold a wide range of opinions and attitudes to Israel. Those who are on the left of the political spectrum may well challenge the State of Israel – and even deny its right to exist as a Jewish state – because, like many others on the political left, they have sympathy for the Palestinians who have so far been denied their own state.

- Many people, especially those on the far left, blame Israel for the fact that the Palestinians do not yet have their own state. Others claim that the main reason for this situation is the way Palestinians have been used by other Arab states to continue their opposition to Israel.

EXPLANATORY BACKGROUND

THE HISTORY

Ever since they were expelled from the Land of Israel by the Romans in the 2nd century CE, Jews have prayed to return there. This does not mean simply the opportunity to live there – individual Jews have always lived there – but to run their own affairs and once again feel it was their own country. Most Jews believed that this was something that would only happen in the messianic age, and so praying for the Messiah to come was the same as praying for the chance to return to the Promised Land.

However, two things happened in the 19th century: the situation of the Jews in Europe became both better and worse. In some countries, Jews started to become more accepted and less restricted. In those countries, the rise of Reform Judaism argued that Jews should try and fit in with the societies in which they lived. Ideas like wanting to return to the Land of Israel might make other people feel that Jewish people were not loyal citizens to their country, and besides, such an idea was old-fashioned and out of date. Reform rabbis argued that modern Judaism should give up these old tribal ideas and learn how to live anywhere in the world.

At the same time, the situation of the Jews in other countries worsened. This led to the hope that the messiah might be just around the corner, and some groups started to organise moving to the Land of Israel in preparation for the messiah's arrival. At this time, the Land of Israel, together with most of the rest of the Middle East, was ruled by the Ottoman Empire. Land was purchased from the Turkish authorities and private land owners, and several new Jewish settlements grew up around the country. Existing communities also grew more numerous in the established towns and cities, especially Jerusalem, Hebron and Safed.

Another group of Jews from Eastern Europe was becoming excited by the new ideas of Marxism and communism. These were increasingly secular Jews who were attracted to the dream of an ideal society where everything was shared and everyone was treated equally. This was a secular version of the messianic dream, and many of these Jews moved to the Land of Israel to set up kibbutz settlements – perfect communist-style villages - where they could live these ideals away from the oppressive laws imposed on Jews in countries like Russia.

As the 19th century unfolded, the idea of nationalism became popular throughout Europe and eventually around the world. Different groups started to dream of – and often fight for – their right to their own political state, throwing off whatever colonial power ran their country to take control for themselves.

Despite the approach of Reform Jews, who were hoping for integration in the countries where they lived, and that of most Orthodox Jews who felt that God would sort things out for them in His own good time, many Jewish people – especially secular Jews – were attracted to the idea of securing a country of their own where they could run their own affairs. In 1897, the first world-wide conference of these Jews took place and political Zionism was formally born.

These Zionist Jews set about lobbying all the world powers to get them on board for this idea. Eventually, in 1917, during the First World War, the British promised that if they won the war, they would help the Jews get their own homeland in the Land of Israel. This was called 'The Balfour Declaration' after the British Foreign Secretary who wrote it – Lord Balfour.

After the war, the League of Nations (a forerunner to the United Nations) agreed to this. Britain was put in charge of the Land of Israel and made responsible for eventually handing it over to the Zionist Jews for their own country. This responsibility was known as 'The Mandate'. The country was called 'Palestine', the name given to the area by the Romans after they expelled the Jews in the 2nd century CE. The Romans abolished the ancient name of the Land of Israel – Judea – to make the point that it would never again belong to the Jews, and renamed it after the ancient enemies of the Jews in the Bible – the Philistines; hence Palestine.

This was a tremendously exciting development for the Jews, and more and more flocked to the country to prepare it for independence.

However, the British then realised that this was not going to be easy. The Arabs who lived in the area did not want a Jewish state in the middle of what was otherwise Arab populated land and they lobbied hard for the British to step back from the idea of a Jewish State. Tensions grew between the two populations and on some occasions boiled over into violence, for example, the massacre of 67 Jews in Hebron in 1929, which brought to an end the centuries-old Jewish presence in that city. In the 1920s, Britain gave three quarters of their mandated land of Palestine – all the land to the east of the river Jordan - to be ruled by a clan of Arabs called the Hashemites. This eventually became the country now known as Jordan. Meanwhile, the British still had to work out what to do with the remaining area of Palestine.

At the same time, the savage oppression of Jews increased under the Nazis in Europe and Jewish people became increasingly desperate to have a country of their own where they could find refuge. When the Second World War started, Britain tried to appease the Arab lobby by restricting the number of Jews who were allowed into Palestine. But as the Holocaust gathered pace, and more and more countries decided they would not accept any more Jewish refugees, the emerging Jewish leadership in the Land of Israel became their only hope.

During the war, the Jews in Palestine backed Britain in fighting the Nazis, even though the British were making their lives more difficult, and preventing Jewish refugees from finding haven there. The Arabs, meanwhile, decided to back the Nazis in fighting the Jews.

In 1945, the full horror of the Holocaust was exposed and the newly established United Nations knew that something had to be done for the Jews. For three years they tried to find a solution that would satisfy everybody.

In 1947, the United Nations announced a Partition Plan, through which the country of Palestine would be divided between a Jewish state and an Arab state. Though neither side was happy with this arrangement, the Jews were desperate to get a country of their own, however small it was, while the Arabs were not prepared to accept this compromise at all.

In 1948, the British withdrew their last troops. The Jews declared the creation of the State of Israel, and the Arab countries around the new state immediately declared war. At the end of intense fighting, the new State of Israel had not only held on to the territory allocated to it under the Partition Plan, but had captured more. From 1948 to 1967, the United Nations patrolled the ceasefire lines, but the two sides continued in a state of constant tension, occasionally boiling over into conflict. In 1967, the surrounding Arab countries – Egypt, Jordan, Lebanon, Syria and Iraq again determined to defeat Israel once and for all. Instead, Israel emerged stunningly victorious and by the end of this six day war had captured even more territory.

By this time, the Arabs living in the area of Palestine were now known as the Palestinians. After the 1967 war, when these Palestinian Arabs found themselves under Israeli rule rather than the rule of Jordan, Syria or Egypt, they decided to fight for themselves and represent themselves. Since then, most people recognise that the eventual outcome will be two countries, Israel and Palestine, living side by side. However, there is such deep distrust and enmity on both sides, that it seems very difficult to work out how to get there.

NB Although Israel is referred to as a 'Jewish state', and it was founded to provide a home for Jews, about 20% of its citizens are not Jewish. Muslim, Christian and Druze Arabs have full citizens' rights and there are, for example, Israeli Arab members of parliament, judges, doctors, diplomats and so on.

DIVERSITY AMONGST JEWS

The majority of Jews today broadly support the existence of the State of Israel, so by that definition, most Jews are Zionists. However, the extent of their support for Israel affects whether or not they call themselves Zionists. For example, they may feel that to call themselves 'Zionists' they must intend to go to live in Israel or actively support it in some way. Every year, several thousand Jews from around the world – religious and secular, Orthodox and Progressive – do indeed immigrate to Israel as a result of their conviction that they want to support the country by living there, or that it is the ideal place for a Jew to live. Unfortunately, many Jewish people also immigrate there because of fears for their safety in their own countries. Recently this has included large numbers of French Jews, due to violent attacks against them in cities like Paris and Toulouse.

At the same time, Jews may support or oppose the actions of the Israeli government at any particular time. One does not have to support the government in power in order to passionately support the right of a country to exist

Although the State of Israel did not start as a religious idea, and Zionism was originally a secular movement, several leading Orthodox rabbis supported the movement and became involved in helping to form the new country. As a result, legal arrangements in Israel tend to take into account, and are sometimes even shaped by, Orthodox Jewish views. Various Orthodox parties play a significant part in modern Israeli politics.

However, Progressive Jewish views played virtually no role in these early stages. As outlined above, Progressive Jews felt that the creation of a Jewish state might lead others to think that Jews had dual loyalties, and the right thing was for Jews to integrate into their own local society. This view took a bit of a battering after the facts of the Holocaust became known, but by then it was too late for Progressive Jews to start building a political base in the soon-to-emerge State of Israel.

However, the 1967 Six Day War changed that. With Israel facing invasion on all sides from its neighbouring countries, many felt that Israel would almost inevitably be wiped off the map. At that point, many Progressive Jews realised that whatever their theoretical view, they felt connected with their fellow Jews, and that the future of the State of Israel was critically important to them. Since then, Progressive Jews have tended to become more associated with Zionism and it is probably true that most Progressive Jews would now describe themselves as Zionists.

Secular Jews, however, have travelled a different path. At first, Israel was the darling of the Left, having thrown off colonial rule to become independent. The kibbutzim were the finest – perhaps the only – example of true communism in action. The commitment of the Zionists to re-cultivating the land had former university professors, doctors and lawyers working as farmers, boosting the status of ordinary working people. Israel was the only example of a culture resurrecting its almost dead language – Hebrew – to become once again a living language of the street. In many ways, Israel was the poster-boy for left-wing politics.

However, as time wore on, and especially after the 1967 war, Israel was painted as an expansionist aggressor. In people's minds, Israel had changed from the little David to the bully Goliath. As the plight of the Palestinians started to dominate the view of what was wrong in the Middle East, more and more people, including secular Jews, regarded Israel as the key part – even the instigators – of the problem. For a long time it was felt that if only the Palestinian problem could be solved, all would be well in the Middle East. Many secular Jews began to feel uneasy and even embarrassed to be on the 'wrong' side of this argument, and it is now true that some of the most vociferous critics of Israel are Jewish.

One of the strangest of the Jewish attitudes to Israel appears in the Haredi world. Generally, Haredi Jews feel that the business of establishing an independent Jewish state should be left to God and the messianic age. That does not stop them becoming heavily involved in modern Israeli politics, but that is only because they live there and want to protect their interests. Israel is constitutionally a secular country, and the Haredim also try to influence the Israeli government to abide by Jewish law as far as possible. But Haredim mostly do not have any ideological stake in the Zionist movement, and most Haredim would probably deny being Zionists.

A tiny section of Haredim are actually anti-Zionist. This small, but vociferous, group – perhaps not more than a few hundred - is often found at pro-Palestinian rallies, Iranian anti-Zionist conferences and the like. This group is so incensed by what they regard as the blasphemy involved in declaring a Jewish State when God specifically punished the Jews with exile, that they feel they must disassociate themselves from it in the most blatant ways.

PROBLEMS WITH THE SPECIFICATIONS

None. Although mostly issues of Zionism are not religious, they nevertheless play a significant part in most Jews' sense of Jewish identity. It would paint an insufficient picture of Jews today if this topic was not addressed.

D.4 THE NURTURE OF THE YOUNG IN THE JEWISH FAMILY

KEY POINTS

- **The family is the main focus of Jewish life.**

- **Many festival practices at home include activities which are designed to involve children.**

- **Bat/Barmitzvah ceremonies mostly take place in the synagogue, but they are major family events. The young person feels the commitment of her/his family to this process of taking one's place in the community.**

- **Generally, Jewish families expect their children to join in adult conversation and discussion. This means that children are inducted into Jewish thoughts and ideas from an early age.**

- **The 'Jewish family' is generally an extended one, and cousins, uncles, aunts, grandparents – even second cousins, your cousins in-laws, and so on – all play a part in family events and festival celebrations.**

- **Because of Jewish history, many families are scattered across the globe. This can further broaden the children's perspective on different Jewish experiences and attitudes, and encourages a global outlook.**

EXPLANATORY BACKGROUND

It is impossible to generalise about families, and every family will manage its own affairs in its own way. This is as true of Jewish families as it is about any others. However, a number of Jewish traditions, practices and mitzvot are likely to result in the emerging of some common patterns.

The innumerable family meals that punctuate the year are opportunities for families to sit and talk; to discuss matters of importance to them and even sing together. Children are included in these meals, and if these take place later in the evening, most families will ensure that the children still take part. In some families, children will be given formal time at such meals to share something they have learned about the festival being celebrated, or the weekly reading of Torah, but the main emphasis is on family enjoyment.

Jewish tradition is comfortable with, and even values, argument - seeing it as a way to tease out ideas and teachings. Children will witness and gradually learn to take part in the cut and thrust of discussions, sometimes on specifically Jewish topics, but just as likely to be about something in the news, politics, art, science or even gossip.

Each of the festivals also provides an opportunity to discuss or teach a feature of the ideas of Judaism – the freedom of Pesach, the giving of the Torah at Shavuot, God's protection at Sukkot, the precariousness of Jewish life but our confidence that all will eventually be well at Purim, and so on. Most families will explore some of this with their children - at the festive table, by taking the children to synagogue, through books on the stories relating to the event, or simply by holding a family gathering which demonstrates to the child that something – even if it is unexplained – makes this day different from other days.

Most Jewish children will attend a Jewish school or weekend classes at their synagogue where they learn to read Hebrew in order to participate in the prayers. In some cases, they learn to understand and speak the Hebrew language. They will also learn Jewish history, mitzvot and halachah, traditions and practices, stories, texts and prayers. They will learn to give tzedakah, and as they grow older they will be challenged to think of the gemilut chassadim they can perform. More advanced pupils might also learn to read and understand classical Jewish texts in their original Hebrew or Aramaic, such as the Talmud and other rabbinic writings, so that in time they can become skilled in Jewish study.

At the age of about 11 or 12, each child will start to prepare for their Bat/Barmitzvah. The actual practice depends on the denomination the family belongs to, but most children will learn the relevant section of the Torah for the week of their celebration. Some children might also be asked to prepare and deliver a discourse to the community on some idea or aspect of Jewish matters that they studied in their year's preparation. Others might embark on a project of research or social action. It is not uncommon for youngsters to twin their celebration with a Jewish youngster elsewhere in the world less fortunate than themselves, and seek to understand their situation. It is also becoming increasingly common for children celebrating this occasion to give away some of their gifts to others, or to donate some of the money they receive to a tzedakah of their choice.

For many young Jews, this might be the last of their formal Jewish learning, but a fair number join youth movements through which they continue to learn about Jewish matters through play and activities. Most of these youth movements are peer-led, so that the 15 or 16 year old becomes a leader in their own right. If the child attends synagogue regularly and is that way inclined, they will soon be encouraged to learn how to lead parts of the service. If they are capable, no distinction will be made between a 14 year old and a full adult in terms of who might lead a service. Indeed, most communities like to encourage promising youngsters to take on as much as they can.

An increasingly common post-GCSE experience for young Jews is a formally organised study tour to Israel for a few weeks in the summer. These are often planned and run by the different youth movements, each with their slightly different ideological views on Judaism and on Israel. About half of all Jewish 16 year olds in the UK go on these trips, which prove to be a formative stage in developing their Jewish identities and understanding. After school, it is not uncommon for students to take a gap year, and some might devote it to higher Jewish study in a yeshivah or seminary, where they study classical Jewish texts intensively for a year.

DIVERSITY AMONGST JEWS

The above outline is somewhat idealised. Although it can be found amongst many Jewish families of every religious stripe, many other families will be more vague about their Jewish position and therefore fail to transmit their values and commitment coherently to their children.

Secular Jews may have a less specific tale to tell to their children. However, they may still wish to pass on their affection for many Jewish practices and will expose their children to Jewish celebrations and talk actively of the Jewish values and commitments of which they are proud. This results in most Jews growing up with a sense of 'Jewish identity', though for some that will be more coherently filled with teachings, values and practices than it is for others.

The one stark exception to the outline offered above is in the Haredi communities. There, the children will start intensive Jewish study at an early age. They are expected to be fluent in Hebrew by the end of primary school, and demonstrate by that age a reasonable competence in reading Bible and some rabbinic texts in the original language. Barmitzvah is less of an occasion, because the boys continue learning intensively. The ideal is to continue with such study throughout their lives. In the Haredi world, there is no higher calling for a man than study.

Batmitzvah is not marked in these communities, but girls also achieve a higher level of competence in their Jewish studies than most of their non-Haredi counterparts. However, they are not expected – and in some sections, not allowed – to study the full range of material.

PROBLEMS WITH THE SPECIFICATIONS

None

D.5 THE WORK OF ONE NATIONAL JEWISH ORGANISATION WORKING TO CARE FOR THOSE IN NEED, SUCH AS TO RELIEVE POVERTY AND SUFFERING, TO SUPPORT FAMILIES OR TO PROMOTE JEWISH LEARNING AND EDUCATION IN THE UK

Obviously, under this heading, schools and teachers can choose any of a huge range of organisations in the UK Jewish community that fit the bill. Below are a few examples that would be of interest and cover the categories outlined here:

Norwood – www.norwood.org.uk – is the leading UK Jewish charity supporting families, vulnerable children and people with learning difficulties.

World Jewish Relief (WJR) – www.worldjewishrelief.org – is the leading UK Jewish charity providing humanitarian support to needy Jewish communities around the world, as well as emergency relief to Jews and non-Jews alike in crises such as refugee situations, floods and earthquakes.

Jewish Care – www.jewishcare.org – is the largest Jewish welfare organisation. It is based mostly in and around London, where the majority of UK Jews live, and provides support for the poor, the elderly and people with a variety of other needs, including mental health issues, bereavement, divorce, unemployment, Holocaust survivors, and so on. Most large Jewish communities around the UK have their own organisations that provide similar services and schools and teachers may feel it is more interesting to look at their own local service provider.

Limmud – www.limmud.org – Limmud is a Jewish adult education and learning organisation, founded and based in the UK, but with sister operations all over the world.

Rene Cassin: The Jewish voice for human rights – www.renecassin.org
Rene Cassin was the French Jewish co-author of the Universal Declaration of Human Rights. This charity works to promote and protect universal human rights, drawing on Jewish experience and values.

Tzedek: Jewish Action for a Just World – www.tzedek.org.uk – Tzedek is the UK Jewish Third World development organisation. It works to alleviate extreme poverty around the world, not just amongst Jews, and to raise consciousness within the UK Jewish community about these issues.

DIVERSITY AMONGST JEWS

All the organisations listed here work and raise their funds across the Jewish community, and have no particular denominational bias or approach. However, there is also a range of denominational groups and organisations that do valuable work, drawing on the specific enthusiasm of their members and adherents. These organisations often do not only cater for their own membership but work beyond the boundaries of their own adherents, especially on humanitarian issues.

NB When Jews work with non-Jews, they do not desire to seek or win converts. Their charity and humanitarian activities are driven only by the desire to follow their convictions about tzedakah – making the world a fairer place.

PROBLEMS WITH THE SPECIFICATIONS

None – though the insistence on national organisations limits the possibility of choosing a local organisation – especially in Jewish welfare work - which might be interesting to pupils and students because of its local angle.

D.6 THE SIGNIFICANCE AND MEANING OF AT LEAST THREE FORMS OF ART, DRAWN FROM:
- **DRAWING/PAINTING**
- **SCULPTURE**
- **MUSIC**
- **DRAMA**

KEY POINTS

- There is a rich history of decoration in synagogues, including painted walls, embroidered cloths and illuminated books.

- One of the Ten Commandments forbids the making of 'graven images' – statues.

- However, Jews have always tried to beautify the objects they use and some of the artefacts used in Jewish practice are creatively designed and crafted.

- There is a long tradition of Jewish music. This music is very varied in style, as a result of the large number of different countries where Jews have lived throughout the centuries.

- There is no tradition of drama in Judaism, in the usual sense of the word. However, there is much ceremony. There is a variety of specific movements and actions set down for particular circumstances and occasions, so it might be said that there is a certain amount of choreography of services and prayer.

EXPLANATORY BACKGROUND

Jewish history being what it is, it is unfortunate that one can only glimpse and imagine what Jewish art might have survived if Jews had been allowed to stay in places longer, or if their traces had not so frequently been eradicated.

In countries such as Spain, Germany, Poland and Iraq, the longstanding Jewish presence came to a brutal end, and the visual arts of those communities can often only be guessed at. Occasionally, one or two examples remain, and provide a small insight into what must have been there when that community flourished.

The synagogues in the Spanish city of Toledo were converted to churches and provide no clue as to how they were previously decorated. But if synagogues elsewhere are anything to go by, these would have been beautifully painted. In Poland, the tiny handful of surviving synagogues, from the many hundreds that used to exist before the Holocaust, are now being renovated. Nearly every piece of wall and ceiling had been covered with pictures of flora and fauna, images of biblical stories or characters, and large amounts of prayer text.

In the late 19th century, many of the well-established communities in Europe built grand synagogues with stained glass windows, borrowing from the church tradition. The motifs of these windows were frequently the festivals, the creation, the tribes of Israel and biblical scenes.

Artefacts which have been preserved from different ages and countries reveal the influence of the host country's style, blended with specific Jewish motifs and concerns. For example, although there is actually no formal prohibition against it, there is a general reluctance to depict human faces too precisely. Nevertheless, at least one of the main Orthodox synagogues in London has stained glass windows with crowds of people portrayed with clearly recognisable faces.

Embroidery enhances many cloths used for religious purposes, including the cloth used to cover the bread at a festive table, the mantles that dress the scrolls of Torah and the curtain which hangs in front of the Ark.

Books and other texts have often been beautifully illuminated and decorated. Popular texts to receive this treatment are the Haggadah (the service book for the Pesach Seder), the Megillah or Scroll of Esther, and ketubot (marriage contracts), which are currently one of the most popular contexts for scribal art. The two key texts of Judaism, the Torah and the Talmud, are never decorated or illuminated. In these cases, it is as if Jewish tradition wishes to demonstrate that the words were all that is needed and require no embellishment.

The second of the Ten Commandments (Exodus 20:4) forbids the making of 'graven images', although it clarifies in the next verse that the real prohibition is against making things one might worship as a substitute for God. As a result, Jews have tended not to make free standing representational models. However, in the Torah, God oversees and clearly approves of the Israelites making images of angels to form part of the Ark of the Covenant (Exodus 37: 7-9).

Jews have always created artefacts, seeking to make them beautiful through attractive and contemporary design. Any website advertising such objects for sale – chanukiot, mezuzot, and so on – will show the wide variety and creativity that goes into designing and making them things of beauty in their own right. This activity is underpinned by the longstanding Jewish practice of 'beautifying the mitzvah', that is, trying to make everything one does for a mitzvah as special as possible.

Jewish music is widely known, and ranges from ancient melodies that are found amongst Sephardi and Middle Eastern Jewry to modern arrangements of traditional prayers. Jewish music has a range of styles drawn from all over the world, but is still influenced by some particular modes and tones.

Synagogue services each have their own traditional chants, as does the reading of Torah. A well-informed person could recognise the synagogue occasion – be it a weekday, Shabbat afternoon, Yom Kippur, etc - just by listening to the chanting for a few minutes. Similarly, the same person could quickly discover whether they had entered a synagogue of Yemenite tradition, East European tradition, Spanish tradition and so on, just by listening for a few minutes. The words of the service would be in Hebrew, and the same in every synagogue, but the chants would be different.

In addition to these chants, there are melodies and tunes for parts of the service. Songs are sung for different parts of the liturgy, and there is a huge variety of styles and moods ranging from lyrical - even mournful - to lusty and joyous. In Orthodox synagogues, where the use of musical instruments is not allowed on Shabbat and festivals, everything is sung without accompaniment. In some synagogues, especially the larger ones, there is a trained cantor who leads the services, demonstrating his (and in Progressive synagogues, her) skilled choice of the right chant and tune for each occasion. Some synagogues, especially Progressive communities, will have choirs.

Celebratory music is also used outside synagogue settings. Wedding music for dancing, table songs sung round the table by a family on Shabbat, tunes for the Pesach Seder etc, all play a part in family life. Klezmer is a highly infectious and lively style of music that was developed in Eastern Europe about a hundred years ago by travelling musicians who provided music for wedding celebrations, and is currently enjoying a great revival.

Hasidic music is another popular source of tunes and songs. In keeping with the Hasidic desire to provide easily accessible forms for ordinary people, Hasidism developed the tradition of songs without words, 'niggunim'. These are easy to learn and enjoyable to sing together, and create a warm atmosphere of togetherness, pleasure and spiritual uplift. The idea behind niggunim is that as long as the singer is in the right frame of mind, the words do not matter; God will understand. It is probably true that when most people refer to Jewish music, they are thinking of either Klezmer or Hasidic tunes.

Other than satiric playlets which have become a tradition of the carnival festival of Purim, drama has not been a developed form in Jewish practice and ritual. That is not to say that Jews are not involved in the dramatic arts, but it does not manifest itself as a form in Jewish tradition.

There are a few ritual steps and movements in prayer, and a number of ceremonies which require a certain kind of 'performance', but it is hard to think of any aspect of Jewish religious life which could be called 'drama', as most people would recognise it.

DIVERSITY AMONGST JEWS

The above is broadly true about most Jews, regardless of their denomination. Progressive Jews might be more open to borrowing from and developing connections between Jewish tradition and the culture of the societies in which they live, but this interest in artistic syncretism and cross-fertilisation is probably only a matter of speed or pace. Eventually, almost all sections of the Jewish world are influenced by the country in which a Jewish community finds itself.

Although this is less obvious in the case of Haredi communities, even they are influenced by the cultural norms in which they find themselves. For example, Haredim in the United States are quite different in manner and speech to Haredim in the UK. Just the name of the Israeli annual Hasidic Pop Contest indicates how this process goes on.

It is also worth mentioning that Jews often play a very active part in the artistic life of the countries in which they live: as patrons of the arts, consumers of the arts and performers and artists in their own right.

PROBLEMS WITH THE SPECIFICATIONS

None

PART TWO
THEMATICS

ACCOUNTS IN TEXTS OF KEY EVENTS IN THE LIVES OF FOUNDERS OR IMPORTANT RELIGIOUS FIGURES, THEIR SIGNIFICANCE AND INFLUENCE, INCLUDING ON LIFE IN THE 21ST CENTURY. HOW VARIED INTERPRETATIONS OF THE MEANING OF SUCH TEXTS MAY GIVE RISE TO DIVERSITY WITHIN TRADITIONS (TEXTUAL STUDY ONLY)

READING FROM THE TORAH, USING A TRADITIONAL POINTER

A ACCOUNTS IN TEXTS

B THE SIGNIFICANCE, IMPORTANCE AND INFLUENCE OF RELIGIOUS TEXTS

C THE SIGNIFICANCE OF IMPORTANCE AND INFLUENCE OF STORIES/PARABLES

D RELATIONSHIPS AND FAMILIES

E RELIGIOUS VIEWS OF THE WORLD

F THE EXISTENCE OF GOD

G RELIGION, PEACE AND CONFLICT

H CRIME AND PUNISHMENT

I DIALOGUE BETWEEN RELIGIOUS AND NON-RELIGIOUS BELIEFS

J RELIGION, HUMAN RIGHTS AND SOCIAL JUSTICE

A ACCOUNTS IN TEXTS

IT IS NOT REALLY HELPFUL OR ACCURATE TO TALK OF FOUNDERS IN JUDAISM, AND GIVEN ITS 3,000 YEAR HISTORY, THE SELECTION OF KEY FIGURES MUST NECESSARILY BE PARTIAL AND INCOMPLETE. IN THIS SECTION I HAVE CHOSEN TO FOCUS ON ABRAHAM, MOSES, DAVID AND THE ROMAN ERA RABBI, HILLEL.

A.1 ABRAHAM

Abraham, together with his son Isaac, and grandson Jacob (also called Israel), are the fathers of the Jewish People. In the biblical Book of Genesis, extensive stories are told about the life of Abraham and his family. I have chosen here to concentrate on two narratives.

In Genesis 17:1-11 and 15-19, we read the founding covenantal statement between God and the future Jewish People. Abraham is told of the sign of the covenant, circumcision, and of the Promised Land.

In Genesis 18:17-33, there is the remarkable account of Abraham's argument with God, demanding that God act morally. This concept is foundational, giving Judaism an expectation that God is the source and standard of morality. God is not there simply to act capriciously or to be able to exercise His power as He sees fit, but that He too is bound by His own standards.

Circumcision remains a widely observed Jewish tradition and is often one of the last practices to be abandoned by Jews as they relinquish other Jewish religious requirements. Jews of every denomination take circumcision seriously, though they might differ in the finer details of how it is carried out.

Similarly, Jews have never forgotten the promise of the Land of Israel, wherever they have been driven or forced to live. It has been manifest in prayers throughout Jewish history, and has informed the decision of many individuals to live there, however inhospitable the circumstances. This drive has become more pronounced in the last 150 years, with the development of Zionism as a political adjunct to the religious conviction.

Overall, Abraham is regarded foremost as an ancestor, not a teacher, and certainly not a founder. When Jews seek to single out Abraham's over-riding virtue, they choose to remember his hospitality.

A.2 MOSES

In the biblical Book of Exodus, three texts provide an insight into Moses, and the way Jews regard him and his story.

In Exodus chapters 3:6-15 and 4:10-14, God gives Moses his mission: to bring the Jewish People (Israelites) out of slavery in Egypt and lead them to the Promised Land. The text exhibits the way in which the family history of the Jews is a paramount feature of their identity. It also shows the model of leadership demonstrated by Moses: modesty and a reluctance to take power when it is offered to him.

In Exodus 24:12-18, the narrative relates how Moses received God's teachings on Mount Sinai and subsequently transmitted them to the people. This is why the most common title for Moses amongst Jews is 'Moshe Rabbenu' - 'Moses our teacher'. However, he is also acknowledged to be a leader and the greatest of the biblical prophets.

Exodus 32:7-14, 30-34 relates another example of someone arguing with God and demanding that He must live up to His own promises, as Abraham did in the story about Sodom and Gemorrah. Despite all the strictures against idolatry, the Israelites build an idol – the Golden Calf - and God tells Moses that He will wipe them out and start again with Moses as the father of a new group. Moses not only reminds God of His promises to the forefathers of the Jews, but also tells God that if He does not keep those promises, he wants nothing to do with the process. Moses stands by the people he has been given to lead.

All Jews generally agree about the towering status of Moses in the Jewish story, and consider the Torah, often called 'The Five Books of Moses', to be a central text. However, almost all the differences between Orthodox and Progressive Jews centre on disagreements about the authority of these texts attributed to Moses.

Orthodox Jews accept the traditional teaching that these words were dictated by God directly to Moses, and therefore warrant meticulous attention and observance,. However, Progressive Jews are more prepared to accept that the text of the Torah is an amalgam developed over time and only attributed to Moses. Their view is that although the text is important, it should no longer be seen as utterly binding, as parts of it would be a product of the times in which they were written. Attitudes, understanding and sensitivities develop and change.

A.3 DAVID

There are three reasons for King David to be considered in this section. First, many of the Psalms are attributed to him. The language of the Psalms presents beautiful Jewish ideas, rich in traditional thoughts and approaches. Second, David's victory over the giant Goliath has provided Jews with hope and pride, even during times of great oppression. The third reason is that David became a king of the Land of Israel, giving Jews throughout history the model of an independent kingdom and an idealised historical moment.

As related in the first Book of Samuel 17:2-52, the story of David and Goliath took place during a time when the Israelites were under the oppressive domination of the Philistines. The nimble, faithful and creative David managed to defeat an ostensibly far more powerful enemy.

In the second Book of Samuel, God confirms through the prophet Nathan that David's descendants will be kings of Israel forever. This promise, which can be read at Chapter 7:8-17, eventually gave rise to the hope of a Davidic messiah who would re-establish God's true kingdom, when the Jews would once again be able to live in peace in their own country.

Immediately after that section, we can read David's facility with sincere, simple prayer and praise. From 7:18-29, the second Book of Samuel provides text which is very similar to the Psalms that are collected in a Book of their own. Almost any Psalm can be selected to provide a sense of their lovely language and straightforward thought. A selection might include Psalms 23, 27, 100, 102, 104, 121, 122 and 130.

David is an imperfect man, but no less influential in Jewish history for that. The Psalms have provided the Jews with a huge compendium and quarry from which to draw ideas and words for their prayers. The story of the lowly boy finding his way to the top through faith and simplicity has always resonated, and his immediate repentance when challenged for a heinous sin is exemplary.

Jews do not regard David as a religious leader or teacher, but he and his story are highly influential and resonate on many levels.

Because David does not appear in the Torah but in later parts of the TeNaCh, the way in which different Jews approach the accounts of his life and activities is less divisive or doctrinally significant. As a result, it is impossible to generalise about how Jews of different stripes might view him. However, the messianic doctrine that is associated with the Davidic line is differently understood by Orthodox and Progressive Jews, with Orthodox Jews typically tending to take a more literal approach to the traditional teachings on the subject (see section C.2).

A.4 RABBI HILLEL

Given that all of modern Judaism might fall under the heading of 'Rabbinic Judaism', it would be wrong to leave this section without mentioning at least one rabbi. There are candidates from across the last two millennia, but we have chosen Hillel. There is an abundance of stories about him and his teachings.

Hillel lived from approximately 70BCE to 10CE and is generally thought to have originally come from Babylon. At about the age of 40, having already distinguished himself as a scholar, he came to Jerusalem and became a leading rabbinic influence, founding a school of thought whose rulings are nearly always dominant. The Talmud contrasts Hillel with another rabbi of his time, Shammai, saying: 'Let a man always be humble and patient like Hillel, and not passionate.

B THE SIGNIFICANCE, IMPORTANCE AND INFLUENCE OF RELIGIOUS TEXTS

THE SIGNIFICANCE, IMPORTANCE AND INFLUENCE OF RELIGIOUS TEXTS AS A SOURCE FOR RELIGIOUS LAW MAKING AND CODES FOR LIVING IN THE 21ST CENTURY. HOW VARIED INTERPRETATIONS OF THE MEANING OF THESE SOURCES MAY GIVE RISE TO DIVERSITY WITHIN TRADITIONS (TEXTUAL STUDY ONLY)

Judaism is a religion of text, but most of it is not easily accessible to non-Jews because the key texts are usually written in Hebrew or Aramaic.

Translations of the Hebrew Bible are readily available, but these are usually an 'Old Testament' with a Christian approach in its arrangement of the books and interpretation of the text.

It is also possible to find translated extracts from the Talmud. However, without an extensive exposure to this huge work, it is difficult to appreciate its remarkable form of teaching and system of discussion, which involved hundreds of contributors and spans centuries of development of thought.

Other sections of this resource cover the way in which texts, particularly the Torah and Talmud, are used to explore and develop teachings (see Sections B.2 and C.2-3) In this section, we will focus on two popular Jewish books and discover the way in which they reveal Jewish concepts and attitudes. Both these books are widely used, and are often found in Jewish homes. They are easily obtainable and will enhance any Religious Education library. Please note that the books should be treated with care, because they contain the name of God and are therefore considered by Jews to be holy.

B.1 THE HAGADAH

The Hagadah is the book used at the Pesach Seder service, which is usually conducted at home around the family dining table. There is a wide variety of attractive and richly illustrated editions, many of which include extensive commentary on the basic text of the service. It would be preferable to obtain a Hagadah with commentary, although the more attractive and accessible the edition is to children, the better.

The word 'Hagadah' means 'The Narration' or 'The Story'; the story in question being the core one for the Jewish people – how God brought them out of slavery in Egypt. However, the Hagadah does not recount the tale in a straightforward way. There is rabbinic commentary on the biblical text and extended riffs on phrases and ideas in the Torah. For example, the Torah says that one should teach one's child about the Exodus from Egypt. "So," ask the rabbis, "how should you teach a child about this?" They postulate four different types of children, each of which requires a different approach. It is interesting to see that two thousand years ago, the rabbis recognised not only the validity of an entitlement curriculum, but also the need for differentiated teaching styles!

The section of the service that deals with the Ten Plagues that befell the Egyptians provides a rich insight into the way Jews might use part of the story to learn several different lessons.

Each person at the Seder will have a cup of wine in front of them, as four cups of wine are drunk during the course of the service. Wine represents joy and celebration in Jewish thought (Talmud Pesachim) but Jews cannot be completely happy if their freedom was obtained through the suffering of others. So at the mention of each plague, a drop of wine is spilled from the cup.

At this point in the service, many will mention a lovely midrash, the traditional way of teaching through homilies, legends and traditions. The Torah relates that after God has split the Red Sea, first letting the Israelites cross safely and then closing the sea to drown the pursuing Egyptian army, Moses and the Israelites strike up a song of praise to God for their deliverance. However, this midrash claims that when the angels in Heaven also started to sing in praise of God, He silenced them. The angels said, "If people on Earth are singing your praises, surely we should, too?" God replied, "In my heavens there will never be rejoicing when my creatures have been killed" (Talmud: Megillah 10b). Simple practices and stories like this teach Jews not to hate even those who are considered to be their enemies.

The Hagadah then goes further, relating how the rabbis played a logic game based on an idea drawn from Jewish tradition. According to this, the plagues God visited on the Egyptians were miraculous events reserved only for that occasion, and will never be inflicted on the Jews. Pursuing the logic of the idea, the more plagues you can demonstrate the Egyptians suffered, the less the Jews will suffer in future.

Three great rabbis then try to estimate how many plagues the Egyptians really suffered. One calculates that it must have been fifty plus ten, another that it was two hundred plus ten. Finally, Rabbi Akiva, probably the greatest rabbi of his time, 'proves' that there were two hundred and fifty plagues in addition to the ten described in the Torah. Although this is only a fanciful game, this small detail of the Seder service demonstrates the pleasure that Jews take in close study of the texts, and the way this facilitates the teaching of new interesting and challenging ideas.

On almost every page, a Hagadah with commentary will reveal other interesting – and sometimes odd – ideas worthy of further exploration.

B.2 THE DAILY PRAYER BOOK - SIDDUR

There are various editions of prayer books, but the most widely used Siddur in the UK is probably the Authorised Daily Prayer Book of the United Hebrew Congregations of the Commonwealth, published by Collins in 2006. It was edited and annotated by the then Chief Rabbi of the UK, Lord Jonathan Sacks.

On pages 418/9 to 422/3 there is a sequence of prayers that is read in synagogue in the middle of the Shabbat morning service, after the reading from the Torah but before the scrolls are returned to the Ark. The first prayer, which was set down many centuries ago, prays for the heads of our study centres. The evidence of the age of this prayer is its reference to the academies of Babylon, which have not functioned significantly since the 10th century CE. This is followed by another centuries-old prayer for the members of the congregation.

Two paragraphs later, on page 420/1, is a prayer for the country and its rulers. Throughout the ages, wherever Jews have lived, they pray for their host countries and governments. In the UK, this prayer is called 'The Prayer for the Royal Family', although it does not take a political stance on the monarchy. In the USA, it is 'The Prayer for the President and Congress'.

The idea behind this prayer dates back to the Bible. When the Jews were exiled to Babylon in the 6th century BCE, the prophet Jeremiah advised them to pray for the country in which they lived and to work for its welfare (Jeremiah 29:7). The version of the prayer in this Siddur was compiled in Britain in the 19th century, but has been updated from time to time. Most recently, the newly appointed Chief Rabbi of Great Britain added the sentence: '...and may He protect Her Majesty's Armed Forces'. In Orthodox synagogues, this prayer is the only one that is read aloud in English.

The last of these is a prayer for the welfare and peace of the State of Israel. This is a new prayer, as the State of Israel was only founded in 1948.

Together, these prayers show how the Siddur and synagogue services are historically relevant, and the way they illustrate the concerns and preoccupations of the community.

Finally, on pages 618/9 – 628/9 there is a collection of Psalms called 'Hallel'. The Hallel service dates back to the time of the Temple, and was added on festive occasions. It is also found in the Hagadah as part of the Seder service. The instructions on page 619, about when the Hallel prayer should be said, are of interest. 'Yom Ha'atzma'ut' is Israel's Independence Day, and although the story of the State of Israel is still too recent for the entire Jewish community to have reached a consensus about how to mark the event in the prayer book, this instruction shows that Jewish practice is still unfolding. The Jewish people continually seek to ensure that their services and prayers respond appropriately to events in their history and their story through time.

Is Pesach historical, political or religious? Is Yom Ha'atzma'ut historical, political or religious? Traditional Jewish practice is reluctant to make those distinctions.

Most of what has been written above will be shared by religious Jews of every type. All Jews use more or less the same Hagadah for their Seder service, although each family decides for itself whether to go through the whole book, abridge it or miss out some sections. In the past, Orthodox Jews would have been more likely than Progressive Jews to enjoy the word play of the rabbis, but this is now changing as Progressive Jews are starting again to appreciate – though not give the same authority to – the traditional teachings of the rabbis.

The Siddur that is recommended here is an Orthodox one. Reform and Liberal versions may not include all of the prayers and may have them in a different form.

Secular Jews are unlikely to have anything to do with prayer books. However, they may still celebrate the Pesach Seder as an act of family togetherness, a commitment to the Jewish People's origins and ethnic traditions and as a festival of political freedom.

C THE SIGNIFICANCE, IMPORTANCE AND INFLUENCE OF STORIES/PARABLES

THE SIGNIFICANCE, IMPORTANCE AND INFLUENCE OF STORIES AND/OR PARABLES THAT COMMUNICATE RELIGIOUS, MORAL AND SPIRITUAL TRUTHS. HOW VARIED INTERPRETATIONS OF THE MEANING OF SUCH TEXTS MAY GIVE RISE TO DIVERSITY WITHIN TRADITIONS (TEXTUAL STUDY ONLY)

As has been highlighted in many parts of this resource, the Torah, the Talmud and other rabbinic codes are used to explore and establish mitzvot and halachah, which are the commandments and the rules by which a Jew should live. However, these are not the only sources of insight into proper behaviour.

First, the Torah does not consist only of mitzvot or rules. It also tells stories and introduces the reader to key figures in the early history of the Jews, as well as others such as Adam, Eve and Noah, who pre-date the Jewish people.

These stories are also rich sources of instruction and indications of the way people should behave.

One example is when Cain, the eldest son of Adam and Eve, murders his brother Abel. God asks Cain where his brother is, and Cain replies: "Am I my brother's keeper?" The answer is an obvious, "Yes". This story is taught to Jewish children at a young age and emphasises the responsibility that people have for each other.

Similarly, when God tells Abraham that He intends to wipe out the wicked cities of Sodom and Gemorrah, Abraham argues with God, begging Him to think of the innocent people who would be destroyed together with the generally wicked inhabitants. Clearly, God has already considered this, but He allows the argument to take place, thereby making it clear that He wants Abraham to think the matter through for himself and, if necessary, challenge Him.

Moses' modesty and humility are depicted many times. One story in the Torah might be selected: God tells Moses that despite leading the people towards the Promised Land for forty years, he will not be allowed to enter the Land. Rather than thinking about his own disappointment, Moses immediately considers the need to appoint a successor. This story is often used to teach the necessary selflessness of a good leader.

In addition to the stories in the Torah and the rest of the TeNaCh, the Talmud is also replete with tales about the rabbis and their behaviour. Sometimes the stories are examples of how not to act, while others demonstrate exemplary practice. In one example, Shimon ben Shitach buys a donkey from a non-Jewish man and when he takes it home, he finds a valuable jewel hidden in the bridle. He immediately returns the jewel to the owner, because it was obviously there in error. His students remind Shimon that he would have been justified in keeping the jewel: the law was on his side, and if the situation had been reversed, he could not have expected the man to return his jewel. But the rabbi teaches them that even though something is allowed by the law, one should strive to behave even better.

Beyond the Torah and Talmud, there is a whole body of material called the Midrash, which is both a compendium of stories and discussions, and a mode of teaching. Something might be 'in the Midrash' or it might be 'a midrash'. Either way, it is a style of reading the Torah and other Biblical texts that draws on long-standing traditions, such as names of characters that are not named in the TeNaCh, or describing events that are not recorded in the Bible.

One example that is widely known amongst Jews is a story about the young Abraham. The Midrash tells us his father was a manufacturer of idols. In this story, Abraham tries to persuade his father that there was only one God, who could not be seen or represented. Unsurprisingly, his father does not want to listen - after all, his livelihood depends on people's belief in these idols.

One night, young Abraham enters the idol factory and smashes all but one of them. Then he places the axe he used to do the damage into the arms of the one remaining idol. The next day, when his father accuses him of destroying the idols, Abraham asks why he is under suspicion when the perpetrator is clearly the idol holding the axe. When his father exclaims that an idol cannot do that, Abraham is satisfied that his point has finally been made.

There are hundreds, possibly thousands, of stories like this. Some are quite fanciful, while others are very telling. The rabbis have no compunction in recounting several stories about the same event that might contradict each other. Their intention was not to create a historical record, but to set down teachings and ideas that can be drawn out of the text.

For example, the Midrash on the book of Ecclesiastes in the TeNaCh depicts Noah emerging from the ark and seeing all the dead bodies lying on the hillside. Horrified, he turns to God and asks: "How could you do this?" Equally angry, God replies: "Now you ask me?" The point is that God would have preferred Noah to try to avert the catastrophe, rather than complain afterwards. The Midrash is claiming that God wants people to get involved, accept responsibility and try to improve the world - and not simply accept God's decisions. This reiterates the theme of Abraham arguing with God in the story of Sodom and Gemorrah. It is for us to remonstrate with God when we fear for our fellows. We are our brothers' keepers.

There is nothing in the text of the Torah that supports this account, and it is not easy to know how ancient a Jewish traditional tale it is, but the Midrash was more or less complete by the early Middle Ages and includes stories and teachings from several centuries earlier.

However, the rabbis did not make up these stories out of thin air, and it is always instructive to consider what may have given rise to the idea explored by the Midrash. In this case, perhaps it may because it is written in the Torah that Noah got drunk after he came out of the ark, and this gave the rabbis the idea that he was distressed by what he saw. Alternatively, they may have used their creative imaginations to imagine how they would have felt in his situation. Perhaps the rabbis wanted to explain why God did not found the Jewish people on Noah, but waited instead for Abraham. What was the difference between these two good men?

More recently, Hasidic teachers have developed a rich strain of tales and teachings. Hasidism was born in Eastern Europe in the late 18th century, and sought to give hope and enthusiasm to ordinary peasant Jews, to assure them that they could secure a positive relationship with God, even if they were not particularly well educated. Through their folksy tales, the Hasidic masters conveyed their teachings in simple language that anyone could follow. Any collection of Hasidic tales will provide further substance to this section.

On the whole, stories are not subject to Jewish disagreement – or to be more precise, disagreement about stories is mostly unimportant. While it is true that some (although by no means all) Orthodox Jews regard the stories of the Midrash as being more literally true than do most Progressive Jews, the meaning and value of the stories is open to discussion. There are rarely any definitive or 'correct' readings. It is the open-ended nature of stories, parables and homilies that provides them with their power and value. An insistence that a story means only one thing would kill the endeavour stone dead. If a narrator's purpose was to make only a single point, they might as well have said that in the first place.

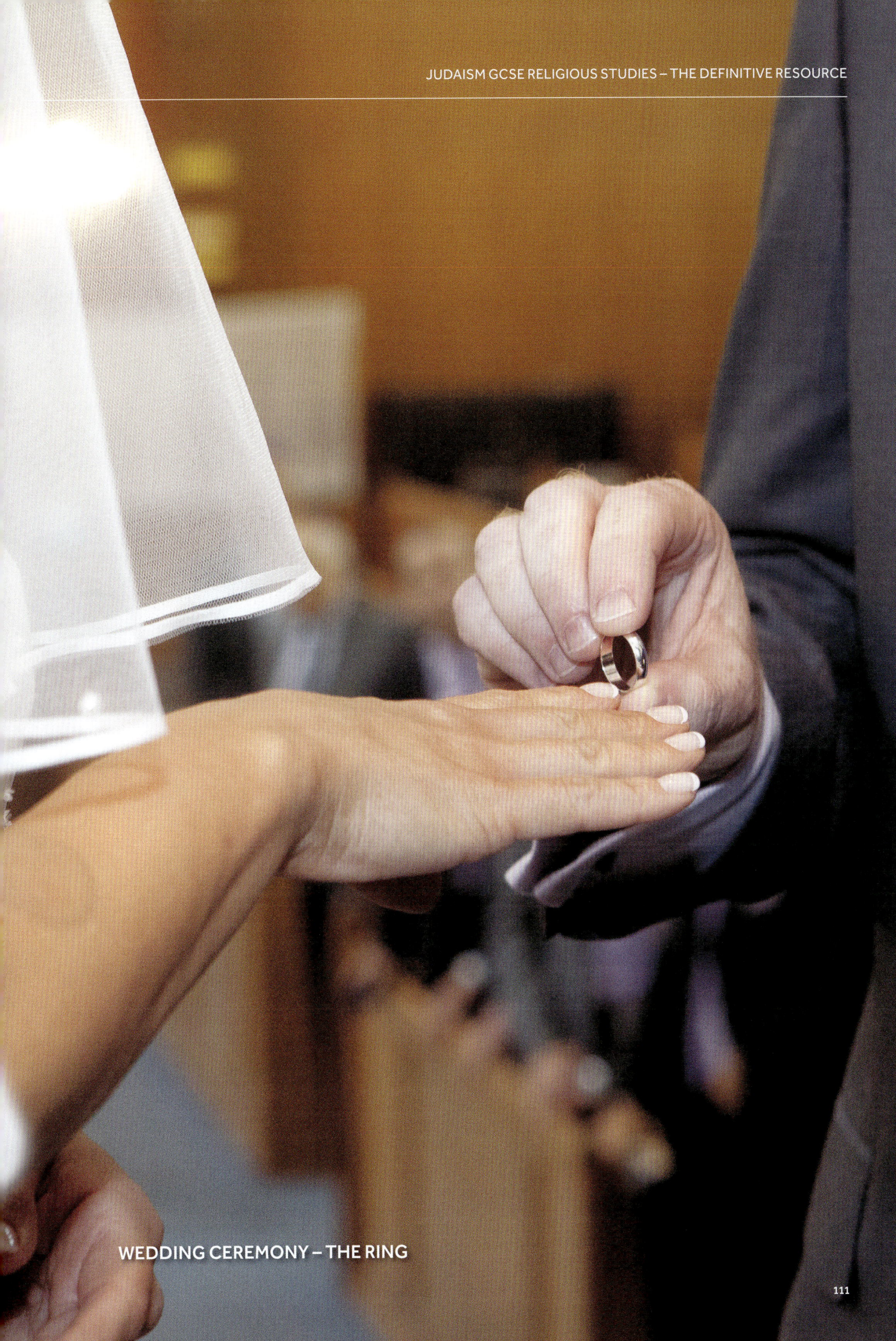

WEDDING CEREMONY – THE RING

D RELATIONSHIPS AND FAMILIES

RELIGIOUS TEACHINGS ABOUT THE NATURE AND PURPOSE OF FAMILIES IN THE 21ST CENTURY, SEX, MARRIAGE, COHABITATION AND DIVORCE. ISSUES RELATED TO THE NATURE AND PURPOSE OF FAMILIES; ROLES OF MEN AND WOMEN; EQUALITY; GENDER PREJUDICE AND DISCRIMINATION. HOW VARIED INTERPRETATIONS OF SOURCES AND/OR OF TEACHINGS MAY GIVE RISE TO DIVERSITY WITHIN TRADITIONS (TEXTUAL STUDY OR RELIGIOUS, PHILOSOPHICAL AND ETHICAL STUDIES IN THE MODERN WORLD)

According to Judaism, the nature and purpose of families in the 21st century is no different to that at any time during the three millennia that the Jewish people have existed. Families are the most secure building block of a stable society, providing a safe environment for the nurture of children, and for adults to care for those they love and for whom they have responsibility. Within the structure of a family, people learn about commitment, love, relationship and responsibility. Family life necessitates selflessness, sharing and forbearance. Those who grow up in a functioning family learn that the world does not revolve only around them.

The Book of Genesis is a handbook of dysfunctional families. Not one generation gets it right and many key individuals get things badly wrong. From the outset, the Torah teaches that family life is not easy.

Rabbis might point to an early statement in the Torah about marriage. The text says that Isaac married Rebecca, she became his wife and he loved her (Genesis 24:67). To the modern ear, this sounds like the wrong order - surely one should love first and then marry? But the rabbis comment that loving before marriage is easy. The challenge is to love one's spouse after marriage. In English, perhaps the difference would be between being 'in love' and 'loving'.

Most Jews do not have arranged marriages; only Haredi Jews have 'arranged introductions'. However, many understand the virtue of a system that does not just rely on the intense feelings of a young person when choosing their partner for life but also considers the way they would fit into the whole family. Indeed, most Jews are brought up to believe that choosing a Jewish marriage partner is very important and know that their parents might be distressed if they choose a non-Jewish spouse. This is not because Jews think that non-Jews are 'not good enough', but because creating a Jewish family will be easier and more likely to succeed if the two partners can participate whole-heartedly in the process, rather than if one is a spectator, however willing. This emphasises the traditional idea that marriage is not just about the romantic notion of two people loving each other, but is also about creating a household and family. It involves parents, grandparents, uncles, aunts and all the other members of the community who have watched these young people grow up and will help them in their lives together.

There are clues in the TeNaCh as to the way people got married in biblical times, but it is only in the Talmud that the process is clearly set down. Marriage is a public commitment freely given between two people. It is also an alliance between two families and Jews have a word – which has no equivalent in English – for the relationship between a person and the parents of their child's spouse.

No-one 'marries' the couple, and traditionally, no-one can divorce them. If a marriage is unsuccessful, the couple divorce each other. It is not desirable, and the Talmud says that God's altar weeps at every divorce. But if a marriage has broken down, it should be terminated as cleanly as possible in order to enable the divorced couple to find new partners and create new families.

These divorce laws have led to a problem which has become increasingly troubling in recent years. The couple has to agree to a divorce; no-one can divorce them or force them to divorce. This means that if one partner refuses to agree to divorce, the other is trapped in the marriage, which prevents them from remarrying. This state of being trapped in a marriage has the Hebrew name 'Agun' or 'Aguna' which means 'Chained One'.

Various attempts have been made to resolve this problem. If they are satisfied that the partner is being unreasonable, the Beth Din (Orthodox rabbinic courts) take out advertisements in the Jewish press in an attempt to embarrass a recalcitrant spouse into agreeing to divorce. The Beth Din also issues edicts instructing communities not to give this person any recognition or honours until they have agreed to divorce. However, these sanctions may have little effect if the individual is not bothered about them. In some parts of the world, rabbinic authorities have persuaded the civil divorce courts not to grant a full divorce until both partners have cleared the way for each other to remarry. Others urge newly-weds to sign a pre-nuptial agreement undertaking to pay the other significant funds if they stand in the way of a divorce. In Israel, where the power of the state can back such an action, resistant partners have been sent to jail until they agree.

However, none of these courses of action is guaranteed. A malicious ex-spouse might be prepared to tough out the sanctions, rather than agree to divorce.

For this reason, Reform and Liberal Beth Dins have cut through the halachic reservations of Orthodox authorities and decided that they will take it upon themselves to divorce the couple if one partner holds out unreasonably.

One reason why this is so important is because of the possibility of producing illegitimate children.

According to Jewish law, illegitimacy does not arise from being born to someone who is unmarried. Although the conventional order of marriage is betrothal, followed by the marriage contract and then consummation, the three procedures might take place in any order. Technically, having sex is just one of the stages in the marriage process, though unsurprisingly, most rabbinic authorities do not advertise this!

In Jewish law, illegitimacy only arises out of a union which is incestuous or adulterous. If a person is still married to their previous spouse, any child they have with their new partner would be illegitimate. According to the Torah, this can have serious consequences on the child's status in the community. As they feel less bound by biblical law, Progressive Jews have largely turned their backs on the biblical consequences of illegitimacy. This makes it easy for them to adapt the laws of divorce. However, Orthodox Jews feel more restricted by biblical injunctions.

The approach to the roles of men and women differs between the strands of Jewish thought. In summary, Progressive Jews have equalised all functions of men and women in religious practice, while Orthodox Jews have retained clear distinctions as to their different spheres of activity and influence. As noted elsewhere, even these attitudes are undergoing considerable review in the non-Haredi parts of Orthodoxy.

However, Jews do not think that men and women should be treated differently outside the field of religious ritual. All Jews agree that men and women should be treated equally; paid the same rate for the same work, allowed access to any job, become eligible to vote at the same age, and so on.

Society has recently become concerned about the way it responds to different forms of sexuality and gender. Liberal Jews, together with the Quakers, were the first religious communities in the UK to conduct marriage ceremonies for same-sex couples before this was formally legalised. Not only did Reform and Liberal Jews have women rabbis from the early 1970s, they accepted openly gay rabbis in the 1980s.

Once again, Orthodox Jews feel more bound by biblical rules. In Leviticus 18:22, the Torah states that homosexual sex is unacceptable and there are very few Orthodox rabbis who would disagree. However, there is at least one Orthodox rabbi who is outspoken about his own homosexuality and asserts that the only prohibition is against penetrative sex. He lives openly with his male partner in a loving relationship.

An increasing number of Orthodox rabbis agree that the prohibition is against the homosexual act, not against the individual. There is no excuse for discrimination towards homosexual people. Furthermore, these rabbis make the point that there are many rules that aren't kept by some Jews, for example, the laws of Kashrut or Shabbat. There is no reason to treat homosexual behaviour as if it were somehow worse than breaking those laws.

E RELIGIOUS VIEWS OF THE WORLD

RELIGIOUS VIEWS OF THE WORLD, INCLUDING THEIR RELATIONSHIP TO SCIENTIFIC VIEWS; BELIEFS ABOUT DEATH AND AN AFTERLIFE; EXPLANATIONS OF THE ORIGINS AND VALUE OF THE UNIVERSE AND OF HUMAN LIFE. HOW VARIED INTERPRETATIONS OF SOURCES AND/OR OF TEACHINGS MAY GIVE RISE TO DIVERSITY WITHIN TRADITIONS (TEXTUAL STUDY OR RELIGIOUS, PHILOSOPHICAL AND ETHICAL STUDIES IN THE MODERN WORLD)

Much of this has been discussed and described in other sections, but for the sake of convenience, a summary is offered here.

Jews take the Torah and other biblical texts seriously, but only Haredi Jews accept the account of the creation as a literal description of how the world came into being. Other Jews have no difficulty in acknowledging the billions of years that it took for the world to develop to its current state, the existence of dinosaurs, and so on. The long tradition of Torah discussion and interpretation allows for non-literal readings of the text, and the rabbinic assertion that 'the Torah speaks in the language of people' (Talmud: Kiddushin 17b, Yevamot 71a) provides a reasonable explanation as to why a text designed to be relevant throughout the ages did not provide a scientific account of evolution to the Israelites thousands of years ago.

The explanations of evolution offered by Darwin and other scientists do not negate the biblical account of creation. The essence of the account in the Book of Genesis is that the world was created with intention, in a particular order and that it was 'good'. Humanity was the crowning glory of that creation, but was also the one thing that God did not pronounce 'good'. The quality of human life will be an outcome of human choice.

The Torah account of the origins of the universe highlights the equality of all Mankind, as well as the difference between human beings and all other creatures. The rest of the Torah legislates for the way animals should be treated and how the Earth should be respected, although traditionally this has been understood to apply specifically only to the Land of Israel. The Torah regulates but allows for eating meat, conditionally encourages agriculture, and so on. Jews today focus on different aspects of these issues. For example, the Jewish Vegetarian Society is keen to point out that, according to the Torah, humans originally were vegetarian. In Isaiah's idealised vision of the future, no creatures will be harmed - presumably returning all humanity to vegetarianism. However, although Jews are required to be concerned about animal welfare, no formal denominations would go so far as to assert animal rights.

God put into the hands of the first humans the power to control the world, which can be understood either as complete licence or complete responsibility. Many translations obscure the subtle choice of words in the original. In the modern age, we are only beginning to realise the tension of the phrase in Genesis that gives the world over to humanity to manage and use (Genesis 1:28-9). Generally, as a result of the traditional interpretations of this line, Jews have always felt that it is their responsibility to seek to improve the world, harnessing their intellectual powers in pursuit of progress and development. For example, Jewish doctors do not worry about the accusation that some medical interventions could be regarded as them 'playing God'. It is obvious to Jews that people should use all their powers to try to improve life. Some rabbis have even suggested that the line 'Let Us make Man in Our image' (Genesis 1:26) is actually God issuing an invitation to humanity to help Him develop Mankind in the best way.

However, like many other people nowadays, Jews are less certain that new developments are always good. Jews can be found across the full spectrum from those who feel that science and technology should be used to improve things to those who would prefer to diminish such interventions and return to a simpler lifestyle for the sake of preserving the planet and its resources. In this regard, the medieval Kabbalistic text 'The Zohar' depicts God showing Adam around the world and telling him that he must take care of it, because if he spoils it, there will be nothing else to fall back on.

Similarly, the Torah tells us that Mankind's curiosity would inevitably drive people from their original simple life to ever more striving, and consequently conflict, jealousy and over-reaching ambition. Science teaches us little or nothing about how to respond to these self-evident truths of the human condition, but equally, the Torah makes no real attempt to inform us of the scientific facts about the way the world works. The rabbis in the Talmud were clear that if one wanted scientific explanations, one ought to ask a scientist – and in their day, most scientific knowledge lay with non-Jewish thinkers. For this reason, while there is a blessing to be said on being in the company of a great Torah scholar, there is also a blessing to be said on being in the company of a great secular scholar. (Authorised Daily Prayer Book p 783).

Section A9 provides full information on Jewish ideas regarding life after death. However, it is worth mentioning here that such thoughts are not nearly as important to Jews as concerns about living life in the here and now. What happens after death cannot possibly be known, but rewards would somehow be bestowed by a good God. However, all sections of the Jewish world agree that the most important point is to live a good life. Although they may disagree to some extent on exactly how this should be done, the principle is to behave well to others and to leave the world no worse than one found it – and ideally, better off.

F THE EXISTENCE OF GOD

THE EXISTENCE OF GOD, GODS AND ULTIMATE REALITY, AND WAYS IN WHICH GOD, GODS OR ULTIMATE REALITY MIGHT BE UNDERSTOOD; THROUGH REVELATION, VISIONS, MIRACLES OR ENLIGHTENMENT. HOW VARIED INTERPRETATIONS OF SOURCES OR OF TEACHINGS MAY GIVE RISE TO DIVERSITY WITHIN TRADITIONS (TEXTUAL STUDY OR RELIGIOUS, PHILOSOPHICAL AND ETHICAL STUDIES IN THE MODERN WORLD)

The starting point for all religious Jews on this topic is the opening line of the Torah: 'In the beginning God created the heavens and the earth'. The Torah does not seek to explain or explore the origins of God, but takes the creation as the starting point for what follows. The Torah is seen as an account of humanity's encounter with God, not as a text about God on His own.

Secular Jews will have a more diverse approach to God, ranging from atheism to a fairly conventional idea that God is an invisible power over the world.

Once again, the Torah is the root text for exploring this topic. It provides an account of God's creation of mankind, and His seeking to instruct human beings in what constitutes the right way of life. During that process, God focusses on one family – the Children of Israel who are the descendants of Abraham, Isaac and Jacob, Sarah, Rebecca, Leah and Rachel. Never forgetting His responsibility for the world and humanity as a whole, God wishes to teach the Israelites to understand and demonstrate what He expects of them. God chooses them for this special role, thereby subjecting them to greater scrutiny and more complex demands. It is because of this that God calls the Jews in the Torah 'a chosen people'.

However, the TeNaCh tells us that God is frequently disappointed in the failure of the Jews to live up to His expectations. Time and again, the Torah makes it clear that although they have been chosen for this special focus, the Jews are not superior to other people.

The task of the Jews is therefore to learn how God wants them to live, and try to live that way. It is hoped that by doing so, Jews will demonstrate the existence of God and His benign influence in the world. This is what is meant when the prophet Isaiah hopes that the Jews will be a 'light unto the nations' (Isaiah 42:6).

All of this proposes an interesting view of God. It suggests that God wishes to develop a relationship with humanity, and presupposes that He understands human beings, recognising that they cannot be perfect. It takes for granted that people have the free will to behave as they choose – otherwise the whole exercise would be meaningless – and that God is prepared to forgive sincere penitents. The traditional Jewish view is of God as King and Creator of the universe, but at the same time He is also Father and Friend. To use the technical terms, God in the Jewish mind is both transcendent and imminent, the still small voice (1 Kings 19:11-12) and the awe-inspiring giver of the Torah at Mount Sinai. Jews insist on the possibility of an intimate relationship with God, while paradoxically acknowledging that He is completely unknowable.

There are two main processes by which God makes Himself known. The first and most influential is revelation. Starting with their receiving the Torah at Sinai, Jews believe that God has been helping them to understand what He expects of them.

As has been noted elsewhere, there is a range of differing views about the nature and accuracy of this revelation, with Progressive Jews doubting that the text should be taken at face value. However, all Jews believe that the text must not just be read but understood, and that it can be interpreted in diverse ways. A student who does not seek access to the Oral Torah, which is the traditional body of interpretation, will fail to understand Judaism or make sense of its main practices and beliefs. Therefore, beyond revelation there is also the on-going process of interpretation throughout the ages, as new issues and new attitudes test the applicability of Torah to contemporary times.

In a famous story in the Talmud, the rabbis are debating a knotty problem. The greatest rabbi takes one view, but the majority of other rabbis takes a differing one. The great rabbi invokes miracles and even petitions God Himself to endorse his view, which He does. However, the other rabbis assert that the Torah was given to the Jews to interpret for themselves, and God could not now interfere. This story was one of the reasons why medieval Christian authorities burned the Talmud for being a 'blasphemous book'.

Jews believe they can come to a reasonable understanding of what God wants, via this interplay between human intellect and authoritative revelations. Alongside this is the phenomenon of prophecy, by which individuals express their inspired insights as to how things have gone wrong and what must be done in order to correct them. However, such prophecies have to be in tune with the Torah, otherwise they are self-evidently wrong and the individual can be identified as a 'false prophet'.

In the main, Jews understand prophets to be commentators on current realities, rather than predictors of the future. Though prophets might warn that if people continue to behave in a particular way there will be certain consequences, these warnings nearly always refer to contemporary events or eternal realities. The prophets are rarely understood to be saying anything too precise about what will happen in hundreds of years' time. Because the prophets tend not to give direct instructions as to specific forms of behaviour, but general prescriptions about broad moral improvement and correction, they are less heeded by Orthodox Jews and are more significant in Progressive Jewish teaching. Indeed, during the first century of Progressive Judaism, it almost turned its back on the Torah in favour of the prophets, but that attitude has now been reversed.

Finally, it is worth noting that the Torah itself cautions against being impressed by miracles, which on their own do not prove anything. The core story of the Jews, the Exodus from Egypt, describes the magicians of Egypt performing miracles. In Deuteronomy 13:2-4 the Jews are warned not to follow a person just because of their ability to perform miracles. The only test of true teaching is in its fidelity to Torah. However, as noted above, the exact requirements of the Torah are open to diverse interpretations.

G RELIGION, PEACE AND CONFLICT

VIOLENCE, WAR, PACIFISM, TERRORISM, JUST WAR THEORY, HOLY WAR; THE ROLE OF RELIGION AND BELIEF IN 21ST CENTURY CONFLICT AND PEACE MAKING; THE CONCEPTS OF JUSTICE, FORGIVENESS AND RECONCILIATION (RELIGIOUS, PHILOSOPHICAL AND ETHICAL STUDIES IN THE MODERN WORLD ONLY)

While Judaism sees peace as the ideal – indeed, it was the Jewish biblical prophets who first articulated peace as the perfect situation – it does not regard pacifism as the best course of action in all circumstances. The Torah accepts that sometimes one has to fight for one's principles. Rules of warfare are laid down in the Torah, which indicate that there are good and bad ways to conduct a war.

The Torah instructs that when one is facing war, one should first seek peace. Nowhere in the TeNaCh is warfare glorified or the status of a warrior presented as the highest achievement. God is sometimes described as a warrior, for example, in the Song of Moses at the Red Sea (Exodus 15:3) but this is only to highlight His power, rather than to raise the prestige of warfare as a strategy.

Similarly, although King David is honoured as a successful warrior in the TeNaCh, for example in Samuel I 18:7, he is celebrated more for his humility, his spirituality and his beautiful prayers, such as the Psalms. Images of King David are more likely to portray him with a harp than with a sword.

Jews recognise that it is possible to wage a war which is valid – even essential. This has sometimes been termed the 'Just War', but Jews may prefer to call it a 'Necessary War' or, in some biblical scenarios, a 'Commanded War'.

The TeNaCh provides several accounts of terrible wars waged by the Israelites, especially those involved in conquering the land, that were directly commanded by God and were conducted under the leadership of Moses and Joshua. However, the rabbis regard these wars as exceptional; they provide few, if any, rules about normal warfare and no wars since biblical times have been claimed to fall into this category.

Apart from those, wars are either considered to be necessary or voluntary. A necessary war is either one of survival in the physical sense, or to ensure the survival of Jewish life and principles. Most of the wars fought by the modern State of Israel fall into the first category. The war fought by the Maccabees in the 2nd century BCE against the Syrian Greeks falls into the second category; it was initiated due to the Syrian leader's bans on circumcision and Shabbat observance, and the defiling of the Temple in Jerusalem. There are also circumstances in which war has to be waged for a simple cause, for example to release captives or to help others. An early example in the Torah depicts Abraham going to war against local tribes who had kidnapped his nephew, Lot. (Genesis 14:12-16).

In such circumstances, the laws of warfare apply. These laws are mostly found in the Book of Deuteronomy, eg Chapter 20. However, the text is augmented by a large body of Oral Torah that explains the way the basic rules in the Written Torah are to be applied. There is no provision in Jewish law for a war of aggression that is simply in pursuit of power or the expansion of territory.

However, despite all the talk of war, the principle of peace remains paramount and is regarded as one of the loveliest outcomes of the hoped-for messianic age. In the Mishnah, the rabbis ask "Who is mighty?" and conclude that it is the person who can master self-control (Avot 4:3). Having power over others is nowhere near as important as having power over oneself. According to the Midrashic tradition, one of Aaron's greatest characteristics was his desire to make peace between people. The rabbis also point out that God Himself blurs the truth a little in order to maintain peace between Abraham and his wife Sarah, because peace in the home is the highest ideal (Genesis 18:12-13).

Jews regard God's tendency to mercy as indicative of the way one should strive to make peace, and to offer forgiveness to the truly repentant. A fair and transparent system of justice allows for society to punish people according to their crime, but after the penalty has been served, the offenders should be readmitted to society. This is highlighted by God's readiness to forgive the sincere penitent, as demonstrated in the story of Miriam being punished with leprosy for her sin of gossiping against her brother Moses (Numbers 12:10-15).

The idea of proportionate justice is summarised in the famous phrase 'an eye for an eye' (Exodus 21:24). Jews have never taken this to mean requiring a physical maiming, but that the punishment should be proportionate to the scale of the crime. For example, in Jewish law it would never have been possible for a person to be hanged for stealing a sheep, as was the case in Britain until a couple of centuries ago. Indeed, if one did take the phrase 'an eye for an eye' to be applied literally, it would mean that someone who had already knocked out two people's eyes could then commit more of those crimes with no fear of further punishment, since they only had two eyes of their own. This is an excellent example of the importance of learning the Oral Torah together with the Written Torah, in order to understand the way Jews seek to apply Torah commandments. A large proportion of Talmud is devoted to discussing what constitutes fair treatment in cases of damage, theft, injury and the like.

Finally, reference has been made in Section A8 to the Seven Noahide Laws. Jews do not seek to convert non-Jews to Judaism, so these laws define the basic decent behaviour for non-Jewish people to be considered 'good'. The seven laws are mostly negative – 'do not kill', 'do not steal' etc, but one is positive: to set up and abide by a proper system of courts of law. According to Jewish thought, civilised society is defined by having a system whereby people do not take the law into their own hands or feel compelled to seek their own justice when wronged.

H CRIME AND PUNISHMENT

CAUSES OF CRIME, AIMS OF PUNISHMENT, THE CONCEPTS OF FORGIVENESS, RETRIBUTION, DETERRENCE, REFORMATION; THE DEATH PENALTY, TREATMENT OF CRIMINALS; GOOD, EVIL AND SUFFERING (RELIGIOUS, PHILOSOPHICAL AND ETHICAL STUDIES IN THE MODERN WORLD ONLY)

Some of these topics have been partially addressed in the preceding section.

In many ways, crime and punishment are the very business of Judaism. Torah and halachah seek to define what constitutes misbehaviour, and how it can be corrected. Judaism does not separate ritual from social behaviour, and therefore views with equal disapproval the breaking of Shabbat and shoplifting. Both actions are infringements of Torah rules, but the difference is that one cannot seek God's forgiveness for shoplifting until the stolen goods have been returned and society's punishment accepted. Another key difference is that shoplifting contravenes one of the Seven Noahide Laws. Not stealing is regarded by Jews to be integral to everyone's good behaviour, whereas the rule of keeping Shabbat is incumbent only on Jews. Finally, shoplifting is against the law of the land, whereas breaking Shabbat is not. A fundamental principle of Jewish law is that 'the law of the land is the law'. The act of shoplifting breaks both the commandment against stealing and that of observing the law of the land.

Jews recognise that misbehaviour stems from two sources: upbringing and personal choice. Parents have a huge impact on the way behaviour is learned. The Torah says that the shortcomings of parents will regrettably be visited upon the children, which is the misfortune of children from weak backgrounds.

However, an unfortunate upbringing does not relieve an individual of responsibility for their actions. Though it may be harder for such a person to behave well, Judaism considers that everyone has the choice and power over themselves to do the right thing. Jews would point to a range of people from similar backgrounds, some of whom are law-abiding and others who follow a life of crime. Neither outcome is predetermined.

Judaism posits that within each individual is a 'Yetzer HaTov' (a Good Inclination) and a 'Yetzer HaRa', (a Bad Inclination). The two sides struggle within us for supremacy, and we can either train the Yezter HaRa to submit to our will, or we can succumb to it. Jews regard the discipline and inspiration of Torah and halachah as great bastions; supporting the development of the Yezter HaTov and the suppression of the Yetzer HaRa in this endless inner conflict.

This analysis explains the Jewish recognition that justice and good social circumstances will help people to behave well. Poor backgrounds, weak education and dreadful living conditions will make it harder for someone to develop their Yezter HaTov. Although individuals should be held responsible for their actions, it should be understood that they were disadvantaged in the battle to do the right thing.

For this reason, it is not surprising that Jews have always regarded social justice as a key aspect of making the world a better place for all, not just for those whom it relieves.

The Jewish fascination with legal ways of resolving social issues means that the issues of punishment and retribution are important, but only in proportion to the crime that is committed. There is also the hope that appropriate punishment will result in the individual amending their behaviour to become a constructive member of society.

Although not directly relevant, it is instructive to look at the Torah legislation concerning slavery and the Jubilee year. The Torah accepts the possibility of slavery; the economic and social conditions were very different in the biblical times for which this legislation was first framed. However, if a person has become so impoverished that they have had to sell themselves into slavery, then the Torah insists that the owner must not only release them after seven years, but must also furnish them with the provision to make their own way in future. Similarly, one is forbidden from taking a workman's tools in payment of a debt. Even if someone has fallen to the bottom of the heap, they should not be condemned to remain there forever.

The Jubilee legislation clarifies this further. Just as is the case today, some people in ancient times were successful or lucky in life, while others were not. The Torah requires that every fifty years all land should be returned to its original owner. It is not certain how this legislation was actually enacted, but the idea makes it clear that people should not be condemned to suffer indefinitely for their mistakes or, more unfairly, for the mistakes made by their parents and grandparents. Everyone deserves a decent opportunity. Although the Torah does not insist on a type of compulsory communism whereby no one is allowed to develop an economic advantage, the worst excesses of uncontrolled, ever increasing inequality are regularly corrected.

This approach can also be applied to criminal penalties. As far as possible, criminals should be rehabilitated and given a second chance. As mentioned in the previous section, God's readiness to forgive is a powerful role model. However, only the person who has been wronged can forgive the perpetrator, even though in criminal matters both the individual and society have been harmed.

The death penalty is legislated for several Torah misdemeanours, but by the time of the rabbis it was clear that they were reluctant to exercise this power. Although they could not countermand a mitzvah in the Torah, they surrounded the rule with so many conditions that it was almost impossible to apply the death penalty in any circumstances. For example, in the case of murder, there would have had to be two independent witnesses who saw the entire incident, the accused must have been warned that he was about to commit murder for which the punishment would be the death penalty, and he must have replied: "Yes, I know," loud enough for the witnesses to hear, and so on. As a result, the death penalty was hardly ever imposed, to the extent that if a Sanhedrin (the supreme court of authority) did issue a death penalty, it became known forever after as a 'Bloody Sanhedrin'.

Having said that, criminals still had the right to be treated humanely and with dignity. Even the body of an executed criminal had to be handled with respect and given a proper burial.

Some of the causes of good and evil can be explained by the free will of individuals and the concept of the Yetzer HaTov and the Yetzer HaRa, as described above. But while that can explain some of the suffering and evil in the world, it does not explain it all. A baby may die an apparently needless death, a good person may undergo hardship and a bad person may prosper, and these remain hard to explain or accept. Jews are convinced that God's world is just and that God is fair, and seek explanations for these apparent injustices.

Part of an answer would be that of life after death. This idea suggests that dying is not the end of life, and things are made fair afterwards. Alternatively, an end of days Day of Judgement will put all things right. However, such explanations are still troubling and many Jews find them unsatisfactory.

A far bolder suggestion can be found in the biblical Book of Job. It should be remembered that it was the rabbis who decided which books would be included in the Hebrew Bible, and are therefore in the Christian Old Testament. The rabbis' decision to include the Book of Job indicates that they thought its content was worthy of attention.

In this book, a good person, Job, is subjected to terrible suffering. He accepts this with fortitude, until his patience gives out and he calls for an explanation. God replies: "You would not understand if I told you. You cannot understand my ways and the scale on which I operate, so there is no point in asking." Job accepts God's answer and the book ends with everything having been put right, and his suffering lifted. Remarkably, the Book of Job confronts this key philosophical issue, poses it as starkly as it can and then refuses to answer the question. That too is part of the Jewish response to the problem of good and evil: we cannot know!

DIALOGUE BETWEEN RELIGIOUS AND NON-RELIGIOUS BELIEFS

HOW THOSE WITH RELIGIOUS AND NON-RELIGIOUS BELIEFS RESPOND TO CRITIQUES OF THEIR BELIEFS INCLUDING THE STUDY OF A RANGE OF ATTITUDES TOWARDS THOSE WITH DIFFERENT RELIGIOUS VIEWS – INCLUSIVIST, EXCLUSIVIST AND PLURALIST APPROACHES (RELIGIOUS, PHILOSOPHICAL AND ETHICAL STUDIES IN THE MODERN WORLD ONLY)

Over the three thousand years of Jewish history, there have been a number of major schisms and divisions, some of which have become quite vituperative. The Torah carries narratives of groups breaking off or objecting to the mainstream, and later in the TeNaCh we see the original kingdom of David divided into two after the death of his son Solomon.

Five hundred years later, Jews returning to the Land of Israel from exile in Babylon found a group living there called the Samaritans, who also claimed to be Jews. There was no love lost between the Jews and the Samaritans, whose claim to be part of the Jewish people has never been accepted. A tiny number of Samaritans still survive today in the Land of Israel.

During the Roman rule, there were several differing views as to the correct way to be Jewish. One group was the small sect of Essenes, who lived in the desert. They believed that God would soon bring about the end of days and warned people to prepare for this doom. Quite a lot is now known about this sect, thanks to the discovery in the 1940s of the Dead Sea Scrolls, a cache of documents and scriptures from the Essene settlements in the Judean desert.

Within the mainstream of Jewish thought, the two main groups were the Pharisees and the Sadducees. The Pharisees were the forerunners of today's rabbis, while the Sadducees were mostly centred on the Temple in Jerusalem and tried to work with the Roman rulers to maintain stability in the Land of Israel. When the Romans destroyed the Temple, the Sadducean view was unable to survive this shock. It was left to the Pharisees and their successors to develop Rabbinic Judaism as the only surviving mainstream school of thought, as expressed in the Mishnah, Talmud and Halachah.

At about the same time, another deep division was created by those Jews who chose to believe in Jesus as their messiah and to assert ideas about him which were alien to Jewish thought. However, that issue was mostly fought outside the Jewish world, as the growing influence of Christianity spread across the Roman Empire.

About 700 years after that, another dissenting group arose. These were called the Karaites, and they denied the authority of the Oral Torah. Some Karaites still exist today, but they are not usually included in the Jewish community and are regarded as a completely separate religious sect.

Hasidism arose in the late 18th century, and was at first considered to be a departure from the true path of Judaism. However, within about fifty years, it had gained so much popularity that it was at first tolerated and then welcomed into mainstream Orthodox Judaism, even though some Orthodox Jews continued to feel that it was wrong in its approach. Meanwhile, a bigger challenge arose with the development of Reform and other forms of Progressive Judaism, which proved to be increasingly popular in the rapidly growing Jewish communities of the United States.

At the same time, the Enlightenment created academic and secular challenges to many of the ideas and principles of traditional Judaism. By the 19th century, there was a large number of different attitudes to being Jewish, ranging from a secular, socialist or even revolutionary position to the comparatively narrow view of Haredi Judaism which distrusts every change or development in the world.

The discovery of other beliefs and fields of research led many 19th century Jews to take on the implications of such ideas and radically adjust their thinking on traditional Judaism. Critics of the Bible posited that the Torah was a composite document, leading the newly emerging Reform Judaism to admit that they could no longer accept that the entire Torah was given by God at Mount Sinai. Orthodox Jews responded in different ways, with the modern Orthodox seeking to resolve such tensions without denying the value of academic study, and Haredim simply dismissing out of hand the findings of such scholars. In matters that do not directly impinge on beliefs, most Jews are interested in the development of modern concepts. For example, both Modern Orthodox and Progressive Jews are comfortable with contemporary scientific teachings about the origins of the universe, the theory of evolution and so on, while Haredim consider such thinking to be wrong or misled.

Alongside this, but less controversially, were the various geographic forms of Jewish practices and customs. These are best represented by the well-known distinction between Ashkenazim and Sephardim, but also include older subgroups such as Indian Jewry, Italian Jewry, the Jews of Ethiopia and the Jews of Yemen, each of which have their time-honoured customs and traditions.

Jews are not strangers to disagreement and division; nor are they strangers to argument. As mentioned elsewhere, the process of argument is widely valued. When debating something of importance, robust and forthright discussion is valued more than being polite. Some arguments can therefore become quite intense, and in many cases one group of Jews will deny the right of another group to present their views as being properly Jewish. These types of argument still reverberate throughout the Jewish world. For example, many Orthodox Jews have little respect for Progressive rabbis and therefore call into question the validity of the marriages they oversee, the conversions they sanction and their right to teach Judaism. Similarly, some of the most vociferous critics of the government of the State of Israel are Jews. There are even some Jews who are in the forefront of claiming the anti-Zionist position that the State of Israel should not exist at all.

So while intra-religious dialogue can occasionally be difficult for some Jews, inter-religious dialogue is much easier.

Jews do not expect non-Jews to convert to Judaism, so discovering what other people believe and creating positive relationships with them is both good neighbourliness and good practice. Jews form a minority within most populations, and it makes sense to develop constructive alliances with the majority. However, the Jewish imperative to improve the world also tends to drive Jewish people to become involved in local and national politics, social welfare projects, charitable activities, etc. Overall, in every age and in every country where Jews have been allowed to do so, they tend to be disproportionately represented in politics, and social and philanthropic activity.

In 1942, the first ever national inter-religious organisation, the UK Council of Christians and Jews, was founded by the then Archbishop of Canterbury, William Temple, and the then Chief Rabbi, Joseph Hertz. These were the darkest days of the Second World War, as the terrible news of the destruction of European Jewry started to emerge from Nazi-occupied Europe. One might see the same level of proactive optimism in the recent founding of several joint Jewish-Muslim initiatives in the UK. These are designed to enable Jews and Muslims to work together on social action projects or simply to meet each other and thereby counteract demonisation and stereotyping. Amongst these initiatives are Nisa Nashim ('Women' in Arabic and Hebrew), Salaam Shalom ('Peace' in Arabic and Hebrew) and Alif Alef (the first letter of the alphabet in Arabic and Hebrew.)

These organisations are not trying to arrive at any agreement or 'truth', nor do they require anyone to compromise their belief. The purpose is for people to explore their common humanity and work together for the betterment of the society in which they live.

From a Jewish perspective, this is easy. Jews do not want others to adopt their beliefs or behaviour. If people are basically good, as outlined in the Seven Noahide Laws, it is not necessary for Jews to try to change their behaviour. More problematic for Jews are the attempts by others to convert them to their own religions. The major evangelical religions of Christianity and Islam believe that their purpose is to persuade everyone to accept the rightness of their position. This makes Jews feel uncomfortable; not only because of the negative Jewish historical experience of such attempts, but also because of the way that these can sour a relationship.

In the main, Jewish attitudes to other people are formed by the way they behave rather than what they believe, so it is not an issue if a non-Jew is secular or an atheist. There are plenty of secular and atheist Jews who express similar views. However, most Jews will feel that there is no reason for the more trenchant atheists to be offensive about others' beliefs, unless an important point can only be made that way.

As expressed elsewhere in this book, Jews are more likely to talk about what they do and the way they live their lives, rather than about their beliefs. As a result, it is not uncommon to attend an interfaith meeting in which the Jews present are not particularly religious but are nevertheless deeply committed Jews.

Within the Jewish world, Progressive Jews will almost certainly identify themselves as pluralist. They generally take the view that there are several valid ways one can be Jewish, and it is not their business to judge between them.

Orthodox Jews range between exclusivist and inclusivist. Haredi Jews will be exclusivist, but although they tend to keep themselves to themselves, both in relating to non-Jews and other Jews who are not of their group, many Haredim will be involved with local politics. They recognise that is the way to stand up for their rights and interests in the modern world, and they will also be ready to help others if an issue comes to their attention. For example, the Haredi emergency medical service will always help a non-Haredi person who needs them. Many Haredim will welcome a non-Haredi Jew to their Pesach Seder or Shabbat table, and there are several Haredi educational initiatives designed to reach out to the wider Jewish community.

Modern Orthodox Jews tend to be more inclusivist. Not only do they strive to include Jews of all sorts of beliefs in their communities, they also try to find ways to work with other sectors – Progressive Jews, secular Jews, and so on. Most Jewish welfare organisations work across the religious spectrum, although Haredim tend only to join these where the numbers are too small for each segment of the community to provide for itself – for example, in caring for children with complex needs.

J RELIGION, HUMAN RIGHTS AND SOCIAL JUSTICE

ISSUES OF EQUALITY AND FREEDOM OF RELIGION OR BELIEF; PREJUDICE AND DISCRIMINATION IN RELIGION AND BELIEF; HUMAN RIGHTS; WEALTH AND POVERTY; RACIAL PREJUDICE AND DISCRIMINATION (RELIGIOUS, PHILOSOPHICAL AND ETHICAL STUDIES IN THE MODERN WORLD ONLY)

Human rights are the heart of the Jewish teaching that all human beings are created in the image of God, as told in the book of Genesis (1:27). This common supreme dimension confers the right to complete dignity for all people, irrespective of their race, religion or gender, and this basic right is not dependent upon them believing in something or behaving in a particular way. Although Jews recognise and celebrate differences, this does not mean that people should be treated differently. This is made explicit in the Torah (Leviticus 24:22). Furthermore, the infinite value of each human makes the illicit taking of a life a monumental crime.

According to the biblical account in Genesis Chapter 1, God created a good world, commenting on each feature as He made it, that 'it was good'. The only creation on which God did not pronounce this approval was humanity. Because of their power of free will, people are always 'works in progress'. Jews recognise that the world often is unfair, and it therefore falls to humans to try to improve the world, or to correct the injustices that inevitably creep into society.

For this reason, Judaism urges Tzedakah, loosely translated as 'charity', to help alleviate such situations. Rules in the Torah, such as those concerning slavery and the Jubilee year, have been discussed elsewhere. In these and similar ways, the Torah sets out a remarkable programme to ensure that inequality did not grow too great, and that would allow people to have regular opportunities to flourish.

Time and again, the Torah asserts that the laws for basic good behaviour should be the same for Israelites and 'the stranger who dwells with you'. However, the Torah does not require non-Jews to observe specifically Jewish rituals, like keeping kosher or Shabbat.

However, this generous and tolerant approach does not mean that everything is permissable. The Torah mandates severe punishment for behaviour that it considers beyond the pale. One example is idolatry, which in ancient times was accompanied by practices such as child sacrifice. When the rabbis were discussing what the Torah intended in certain circumstances, their understanding of the objection to idolatry was not the attempt to depict God, but the practices associated with these fearsome beliefs. For example, the Jews would have considered the statues of gods and goddesses in the Ancient Greek tradition to be wrong in principle, but most Jews did not criticise Greek practices and actually found much to admire in their science and philosophy. It was only when there was an attempt to force the Jews to adopt the Greek traditions, that they resisted and eventually revolted.

Though the modern State of Israel is a liberal democracy and is not driven by Jewish law, Jewish attitudes influence many of its approaches and its legal system. Noticeable in this regard is the acceptance of a wide range of religious beliefs, incorporating them into the laws of the country. For example, all marriages performed by Jews, Christians, Muslims and some other religions are considered valid, without the need of any further civil ceremony. A variety of religious festivals, in addition to the Jewish ones, are protected under the law as public holidays, and the holy places of Jews, Christians, Muslims and Baha'is are equally safeguarded.

This tolerance is also shown in areas beyond religion. Homosexuality is legal, and Israel has the most free gay scene of any country in the Middle East. Although homosexual acts are still considered taboo in Orthodox Judaism, the Gay Pride Parades in Israel are large public events, protected and managed by the police and widely reported by the media. In 1998, the transgender singer Dana International won the Eurovision Song Contest for Israel. Women's equal rights have been enshrined in the law since Israel was founded.

Of course, this does not make Israel or the Jewish people perfect in regard to prejudice and discrimination. All societies prefer 'their own' and make distinctions within their own populations, with one group or another being looked down on and disadvantaged. In this regard, Jews are no different from anyone else. This section merely clarifies that within Jewish teaching and tradition, the tools exist to challenge such negative tendencies.

Organisations in the UK use these teachings and values to challenge the Jewish community to raise its game. JCORE – the Jewish Council for Racial Equality - is one such organisation, as is René Cassin, UK Jewry's human rights pressure group. Jews were in the forefront of the civil rights movement in the United States in the 1960s, seeking to secure equal rights for Black Americans, and they were represented disproportionately in the anti-apartheid movement both within and outside South Africa during its years of apartheid. It might be argued that since Jews have so often been at the receiving end of discrimination, their antennae are more sensitively tuned to it than those who may not have suffered in this way.

For similar reasons, Jews were generally enthusiastic about socialism and communism at the end of the 19th century, because they saw in it a way to bring more fairness to the world. Kibbutzim, the agricultural settlements in the land of Israel that predated the establishment of the state, were the purest examples of communities living fully according to socialist values. On the kibbutz, there was no private property, all profits were equally shared, dining was communal, children were brought up together by the community and decisions were made by all members at meetings. Not all the kibbutzim were religious, and indeed some were actively anti-religious, but there were many Orthodox kibbutzim that sought a way to bring together the ideals of communism and Orthodox Jewish practice.

Finally, racial prejudice has no place in Jewish thought, although Jews are no more perfect than any other group of people and might fall victim to such attitudes. Based on the principle with which this section opened, all human beings are created in the image of God and discrimination on the basis of a person's appearance cannot be justified. Similarly, absolute need has to be responded to regardless of who is suffering. Tzedek, the Jewish Third World poverty relief agency, works only with non-Jewish communities as they are currently those who are subjected to the deepest poverty. World Jewish Relief, UK Jewry's emergency relief organisation, raises funds and provides aid to victims of earthquakes, flood and other disasters, regardless of whether or not such communities feel positively towards Jews. IsraAid, Israel's emergency relief organisation, similarly provides help to crises around the world, regardless of whether or not that country has diplomatic relations with Israel. Humanity must never be overlooked because of current politics.

Like all other groups, Jews differentiate between themselves and others, but differentiation is not the same as discrimination. In Jewish terms, this differentiation leads to a sense of solidarity between Jews, whatever their racial type or lifestyle. For example, during the Ethiopian famines about thirty years ago, while other countries tried to help the millions of Ethiopians threatened with starvation, and Jews the world over donated money and aid to alleviate their suffering, the Israeli government arranged for as many Ethiopian Jews as possible to be airlifted to Israel, where they were given a new life. The colour of their skin was of no consequence. They were Jews and therefore had to be helped.

THE BOARD OF DEPUTIES OF BRITISH JEWS

GLOSSARY AND FURTHER RESOURCES

BATMITZVAH GIRL IN REFORM SYNAGOGUE

GLOSSARY

MOST WORDS ENDING IN A CONSONANT HAVE A PLURAL ENDING '-IM';

EG HASSID/HASSIDIM

MOST WORDS ENDING IN '-AH' HAVE A PLURAL ENDING '-OT';

EG MITZVAH/MITZVOT

MANY WORDS ENDING IN '-T' ARE COMMONLY WRITTEN IN ENGLISH AS ENDING IN '-TH';

EG MITZVOTH

'CH' IS ALWAYS PRONOUNCED GUTTURALLY, AS IN 'LOCH'. IT IS SOMETIMES ALSO SPELLED 'KH' OR SIMPLY 'H';

EG HANUKAH

Adonai	lit. My Lord. The word used to replace the unutterable four letter name of God
Agun/Aguna	lit. Chained person. Someone refused a divorce by their spouse
Amidah	lit. Standing prayer. The central prayer of every statutory service
Aron Hakodesh	lit. Holy Ark. The cupboard, often ornate, which houses the Torah scrolls
Ashkenazi	Jews of the northern European tradition, often called 'German and Polish'
Avodah	lit. Work/Service. Now also come to mean 'worship'
Ayn Sof	lit. Without limit. One of the descriptive names given to God
Barmitzvah	lit. Son of the mitzvot. The coming of age event for a boy at thirteen years old
Batmitzvah	lit. Daughter of the mitzvot. The coming of age event for a girl at twelve years old
BCE	Before the Common Era. Equivalent to BC, which is a Christian definition of time
Beth Din	lit. House of Law. A rabbinical court of at least 3 rabbis
Be'tzelem Elohim	lit. In the image of God. The concept underpinning human equality
Bikur Cholim	lit. Visiting the sick. By extension, the whole field of health care and medicine
Bimah	lit. Platform. The raised platform in a synagogue from which the service is led
Brit Milah	lit. Covenant of Circumcision. The circumcision ceremony for boys at eight days old
CE	The Common Era. Equivalent to AD, which is a Christian definition of time
Chabad Lubavitch	A hasidic sect, sometimes called by either word on its own
Chessed	lit. Kindness. The virtue of caring
Chumash	lit. Five. A printed book of the Written Torah – the Five Books of Moses
El Shaddai	lit. God Almighty. One of the descriptive names given to God
Gemarah	lit. Completion. The main body of the Talmud, containing extensive rabbinic debate
Gemillut Chasadim	lit. Acts of kindness. The whole field of doing good to others

Get	lit. Divorce. Now also applied to the divorce document
Hagadah	lit. The narration. The service book for the Pesach Seder service
Halachah	lit. The way to go. The agreed view on how to fulfil a mitzvah
Hallah	A rich doughy bread, often plaited, used for Shabbat and festivals
Hallel	lit. Praise. A sequence of psalms sung on festival occasions
Hanukah	lit. Dedication. The eight day festival in Nov/Dec celebrating the rededication of the Jerusalem Temple in about 162BCE
Hanukiah	The eight branch candlestick (with an extra branch) used at the festival of Hanukah
Huppah	The wedding canopy under which a marriage ceremony takes place
Ha'rahaman	lit. The Merciful One. One of the descriptive names given to God
Haredi	lit. Trembling one. One who adheres to a separatist approach to Judaism
Hassid	lit. Righteous one. One who adheres to the charismatic mystical Hassidic approach
Havdalah	lit. Distinction. The ceremony marking the end of Shabbat and festivals
Holocaust	lit. Burnt offering. The systematic attempt at genocide of the Jews by the Nazis during WWII, killing 7/8 of European Jews
Kabbalah	lit. Received material. The mystical Jewish tradition
Kashrut	lit. Permissibility. The body of rules determining acceptability in Jewish law
Ketubah	lit. Written document. A marriage contract
Ketuvim	lit. Writings. The third section of the TeNaCh
Kibbutz	lit. A gathering. Zionist socialist settlements in Israel
Kiddush	lit. Sanctification. The prayer said over wine to declare and celebrate a holy day
Kippa	A small brimless cap of any design used to cover the head as a sign of respect to God
Klezmer	Joyous wedding music originating in 19th century eastern Europe
Kosher	Acceptable according to Jewish law. See 'Kashrut'
Lulav	lit. Palm branch. Now applied to the four tree items waved on Sukkot

Maccabees	lit. Hammers. Family name given to those who defeated the Syrian Greek occupation of Jerusalem and the Temple in the 2nd century BCE
Magen David	lit. Shield of David. A six pointed star
Masorti	lit. Traditional. One who adheres to the Masorti denomination
Matzah	Unleavened bread. Especially significant at Pesach
Megillah	lit. A scroll. Especially used to identify the Book of Esther used at Purim
Menorah	lit. A lamp. Especially used to identify the seven branched candlestick used in the Temple
Messiah	lit. Anointed one. The anticipated leader who will inaugurate a golden age
Mezuzah	lit. Doorpost. The finger-sized box with biblical texts inside fixed to the doorpost
Midrash	lit. Homiletic story. Early medieval compendium of rabbinic homiletic teachings – The Midrash. One such teaching – a midrash
Minyan	The quorum of ten required for full congregational prayer services
Mishnah	lit. Repetition. The core of the Talmud, completed in about 200CE
Mitzvah	lit. Commandment. Including also the sense of a good deed and a meritorious act
Ner Tamid	lit. Everlasting light. A light left on continuously near the Aron Hakodesh
Nevi'im	lit. Prophets. The second section of the TeNaCh
Noahide Laws	lit. Laws of Noah. A rabbinic teaching as to the seven laws that are the basic components of a moral life for all people
Parev/Parve	'Neutral' foods, neither dairy nor meat, such as vegetables, fruit, fish and eggs
Pesach	The spring festival of Passover, commemorating the Exodus from Egypt
Pikuach Nefesh	lit. Looking after a soul. The principle that saving life overrides nearly everything
Purim	An early spring carnival festival celebrating the saving of the Jews of Persia
Rabbi	lit. My teacher. An individual with high levels of Jewish learning able to make rulings
Rebbe	The leader of a Hasidic sect, usually dynastic. Often considered to have remarkable levels of spiritual capacity

Rosh Hashanah	lit. Head of the Year. New Year festival falling in September/October
Shechitah	The kosher system of slaughtering meat, to cause the least pain and drain the maximum of blood from the carcass
Seder	lit. Order. The festive meal/service which takes place at the beginning of Pesach
Sephardi	Jews of the Mediterranean tradition, often called Spanish and Portuguese
Shabbat	lit. Rest day. The weekly festive day of rest, from Friday evening till Saturday evening
Shavuot	lit. Weeks. The early summer festival, 50 days after Pesach, also called Pentecost
Shechinah	lit. The Indwelling. The idea of God as a particularly intense presence
Shema	lit. Listen. The declaration of faith in one God, from the Torah
Shivah	lit. Seven or Sitting. The 7 day period of intense mourning by the bereaved after a death
Shofar	An animal horn (usually a ram's horn) blown on Rosh Hashanah
Siddur	lit. Orderly book. A prayer book
Simchat Torah	lit. Celebration of the Torah. Autumn festival marking the end and beginning of the year-long cycle of reading the Torah
Sukkah	The loosely roofed hut used during the festival of Sukkot
Sukkot	The autumn harvest festival
Synagogue	lit. Meeting place (Greek). The Jewish community, learning and prayer centre
Tallit	A large scarf or cloak, carrying the commanded four fringes on the corners, worn at morning services
Talmud	lit. Study text. A huge compendium of rabbinic debate on Jewish teachings
Tefillin	lit. Prayers. Black leather prayer aids containing texts from Torah, worn on head and arm during weekday morning services
TeNaCh	The acronym used for the Hebrew Bible, based on its three parts
Tikkun Ha'olam	lit. Repairing the world. Now come to mean the full range of social action work
Tisha b'Av	lit. 9th of Av. Midsummer 25 hour fast mourning the fall of the Temple

Torah	lit. Teaching. The first five books. Also the corpus of Jewish teaching and tradition
Trefah	lit. Torn. By extension, all non-kosher food
Tzedakah	lit. Fair action. Usually used to describe charity
Tzitzit	The fringes on the corners of a garment, as commanded in Torah
Yeshivot	lit. Sitting places. Centres of higher Jewish learning. (sing. Yeshivah)
Yetzer HaTov/ Yetzer HaRa	lit. The good/evil inclination. The idea that within each person are warring
Yom Ha'atzma'ut	lit. Day of Independence. The festive day marking Israel becoming an independent State following the UN vote in 1948
Yom Kippur	The Day of Atonement. A full 25 hour fast devoted to repentance
Zionist	One who believes that the Jews should have their own country in the land of Israel
Zohar, The	lit. Splendour. A medieval book of Jewish mysticism. The main text of kabbalah